LOCOMOTION PAPERS

Goodbye to Victoria
The Last Queen Empress

*The Story of Queen Victoria's
Funeral Train*

by
Peter J. Keat

THE OAKWOOD PRESS

© Oakwood Press & Peter J. Keat 2001

British Library Cataloguing in Publication Data
A Record for this book is available from the British Library
ISBN 0 85361 569 1

Typeset by Oakwood Graphics.
Repro by Ford Graphics, Ringwood, Hants.
Printed by Inkon Printers Ltd, Yateley, Hants.

LB&SCR locomotive No. 54 *Empress* dressed and decorated for a festive occasion.

Title page: Queen Victoria travels in the London & North Western Railway Royal Train with her daughter Princess Beatrice, as a Lady in Waiting looks on.

Front cover: An original painting by Murray Secretan of Queen Victoria's funeral train hauled LB&SCR 4-4-0 No. 54 *Empress.*   *Oakwood Press*
Rear cover: Four generations of the Royal Family, Queen Victoria (*centre*), with to her left grandson George (later King George V), to her right her son Edward (later King Edward VII), and in the foreground her great-grandson Edward (later King Edward VIII).

Published by The Oakwood Press (Usk), P.O. Box 13, Usk, Mon., NP15 1YS.
E-mail: oakwood-press@dial.pipex.com
Website: www.oakwood-press.dial.pipex.com

Contents

The Royal Mausoleum, Frogmore.   *The Sphere*

Her Majesty Queen Victoria.

Introduction

'All day long the Angel of Death has been hovering over Osborne House. One could almost hear the beating of the wings, but at a quarter past six those wings were folded and the Queen was at rest'. These words were written by the Special Court correspondent of *The Times* on 22nd January, 1901, the day Queen Victoria died. Naturally all British newspapers carried this as their main story, but what was surprising was the widespread coverage by newspapers from other countries. For example, the *New York Tribune* featured the story on the whole of its front page with pictures of the late Queen and new King Edward over the legend 'The Queen is dead. Long live the King'. It went on to describe the nation's grief and sorrow, the massive wave of sympathy which was sweeping the country, the tributes from not only all over Europe but from countries and nations worldwide and here, at home in Britain, the hasty recall of both the Houses of Parliament to the Palace of Westminster.

Straightaway plans began to be laid for one of the most unusual and remarkable railway journeys in history. Three different locomotives from three different railway companies hauled the train carrying the body of the late Queen from the Royal Clarence Yard in Gosport to London Victoria, and then from Paddington to Windsor. Because of the number of crowned heads and other Royal and important personages on the train along with all the security implications, the authorities decided that no photographers would be allowed access to any part of the route. The whole length of all the lines the Royal Train traversed was patrolled by specially delegated railway employees. The result of this was that any photographs of the Royal Funeral train are very rare and so far, after years of searching, the author has only had a handful come into his possession. But more of the funeral journey and arrangements later, firstly what were the main events of the last few weeks of her life which led up to Queen Victoria's death?

Possibly the last painting of Victoria. This portrait by Stanford J. Stanford was unfinished at the time of the Queen's death.

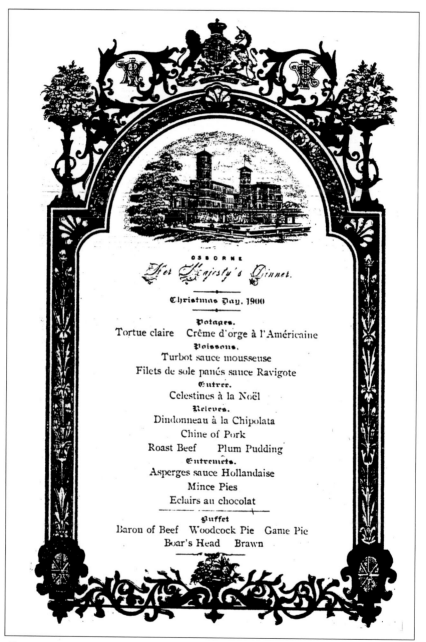

OSBORNE

Her Majesty's Dinner.

Christmas Day, 1900

Potages.
Tortue claire   Crême d'orge à l'Américaine
Poissons.
Turbot sauce mousseuse
Filets de sole panés sauce Ravigote
Entrée.
Celestines à la Noël
Relevés.
Dindonneau à la Chipolata
Chine of Pork
Roast Beef   Plum Pudding
Entremets.
Asperges sauce Hollandaise
Mince Pies
Eclairs au chocolat

Buffet
Baron of Beef   Woodcock Pie   Game Pie
Boar's Head   Brawn

Christmas Day menu Osborne House 1900. One hopes that this was the menu that was set before the members of the Royal Family and not before a Queen who by now abhorred the sight of food.

Chapter One

Background

The last year of the 19th century had been a busy one for the ageing and ailing Queen. She had paid an official visit to Ireland, heard of the relief of Mafeking and the death of both her son, Alfred, the Duke of Edinburgh (known to the family as Affie), from cancer, and Prince Christian Victor of Schleswig-Holstein (known to the family as Christle) from enteris fever whilst serving in Pretoria, South Africa. One of the last Royal duties which she was to perform was to bestow the Order of the Garter on the military leader Lord Roberts. (The author is proud to point out that during this period of time his grandfather was Lord Roberts' personal bugle boy.)

By the turn of the century it was obvious to those close to her that the Queen was ageing fast. She was in her early eighties and had developed a tendency to doze during the day because she suffered very badly from insomnia.

In her Journal of 11th November she wrote 'Had a shocking night, and no draught could make me sleep, as the pain kept me awake. Felt very tired and unwell when I got up . . . could do nothing for the whole morning. Rested and slept a little'. The pain to which the Queen referred was quite possibly severe rheumatism, an affliction from which she suffered a great deal in her later life.

Rheumatism was not her only medical problem, she also suffered with digestive problems. But despite this she insisted on eating large hearty meals for most of her life and when the gastric problems hit, she refused to steer clear of roast meats and other rich foods and concentrate on chicken and other forms of lighter fare. In fact when the Queen's Royal Physician, Sir James (later Lord) Reid, suggested that for her digestion's sake she should take 'Bengers' once a day, this she did, but not as was suggested as a replacement for a meal but as an addition to it. However by the time she arrived in Osborne House the whole situation had changed. Over the last few weeks of her life her desire for food had diminished to practically nothing and now the sight of food repelled her.

Mental anxiety was also taking its toll on the Queen's health. She was deeply concerned about the progress of the Boer War. She worried about the loss of life and the number of wounded troops and the effect that death and injury had on the new widows and families left at home. She felt she had a fellow feeling as she herself was a widow and a mother who had lost a child, and especially as she had also recently lost a grandson in that South African campaign. She was also very worried about the Irish problem and had, in the previous summer, insisted on visiting that country and so making it possible for her to be seen by her subjects. The tour was a severe strain on her and she returned home exhausted and drained.

The Queen's eyesight was also something which was giving the Royal Family much cause for concern as it had been failing fast over the last few years. In fact, by Christmas 1900, she had to be helped to sign official documents, although the Queen refused to admit that she was having any difficulties. When, on Christmas Eve, she was taken, as was the custom, into the Durbar Room in

. . . SELECTION OF MUSIC . . .

1. TRIUMPHAL MARCH   " Virtute et Valore."   *L. Zavertal*
2. OVERTURE   ...   " Raymond."   ...   *Thomas*
3. " MENUET "   ...   .   *Paderewski*
4. SELECTION   ...   " Shamrock."   ...   *L. Zavertal*
5. " TOREADOR ET ANDALOUSE   ...   ...   *Rubinstein*
      (From the Suite " Bal Costumé.")
6. (a) Anitra's Dance   ...   .
    (b) Dance in the Hall of the King of the Mountains   ...   }   *Grieg*
      (From the Suite " Peer Gynt.")
7. GRACEFUL DANCE (" from Henry VIII.")   .   ...   *Sullivan*
8. OVERTURE   ...   " Ruy Blas."   ...   *Mendelssohn*

Buckingham Palace,   *Conductor*—CAV. L. ZAVERTAL, R.A.
January 3rd, 1901.

The music selection played at Christmas Day dinner, despite the date and venue in the bottom left-hand corner of the card.

The Sphere

Osborne House to view the Royal Christmas tree she complained that the tree, which was brilliantly lit, was so dull she could hardly see it. For many years she had delighted in trimming the Christmas tree herself. The Durbar Room was so often the venue for the plays and tableaux which were performed on a specially built stage with theatrical lighting, by the members of the Royal Family and the household. The Queen always attended every rehearsal of each production.

By the time that the Christmas season had come in 1900 the Queen's bouts of insomnia were getting worse and worse and she had been prescribed Charol to help her relax and to sleep. However, an unfortunate side effect soon took hold. This was the prolonged feeling of drowsiness when she woke up and progressively it took the Queen most of the morning to sleep off the effects of the drug. It was now becoming obvious to the Royal Family and the members of the household resident in Osborne House that Christmas 1900 was going to be a quiet and somewhat joyless affair.

To compound the depressing situation on Christmas Day the Queen was informed that her beloved Lady in Waiting, Lady Jane Churchill, had passed away that morning. Lady Jane had been in Royal service for over 46 years and the Queen was most distraught when she heard the sad news. By now the Queen's doctor on his own initiative telegraphed his serious concerns to her eldest son Prince Edward, the Prince of Wales.

The last day of the old year (and century) dawned and the Queen's health was still causing concern. Most of her life the Queen had kept a diary and on that day she wrote: 'A terrible stormy night. The same alternations of sleep and restlessness, so again I do not get up when I wished to, which spoilt my morning and day. Got out a little after one o'clock with Beatrice (her daughter). The afternoon was wet and I took a short ride in a closed carriage'.

New Year's Day saw the Queen in no better health or humour and it was obvious that she did not face the prospect of a New Year with any enthusiasm or commitment. The first line in her journal of that year said 'Another year begun and I am feeling so weak and unwell that I enter upon it sadly'. Later she rallied and on the following day she was well enough to admit Lord Roberts as a Knight of the Order of the Garter. Later, when the new Garter Knight was asked about the health of the Queen, he remarked how frail and infirm he thought she had looked.

Just over a week later the Queen must have been in much better health because on 10th January she wrote in her diary that she had had a rather better night but had slept late. She must have felt somewhat improved because she was well enough to take a carriage drive to Newport accompanied by her daughter Princess Beatrice. It was during one of these drives into town that she eventually confided to her daughter that she thought her death was not too far away and that she would soon be reunited with her beloved Albert.

Some of the business of State (the infamous red boxes which are still prevalent today) occupied her two days later when, having had a good night's rest and taken some breakfast, she granted a 20 minute audience to the Prime Minister, Mr Joseph Chamberlain. He was in fact the last Minister to see the Queen alive and he remarked how she had a good clear complexion and was bright eyed. Later that day she again took a short drive in and around the grounds of Osborne House.

The following day, Sunday 13th January, 1901, the Queen wrote that she had a fair night and managed to get up earlier and drink some arrowroot and milk. She managed to take short drives during the day and at 5.30 she went down into the drawing room where a short service was held by the Rector of Whippingham, the Revd Canon Clement Smith. The Queen was much impressed with the service and afterwards she retired and managed to sign some more state documents. The notes regarding her night's sleep and the breakfast milk were the final entries in her diary, a journal which she kept faithfully for almost 70 years. Surely the fact that she did not continue to write it was a strong indicator of her health and state of mind.

The next day, Monday 14th, she saw Lord Roberts and discussed the situation and good news of victory in South Africa. To him she seemed bright and the audience lasted for over an hour. But to those who were close and knew the Queen realised that she hardly knew where she was. It is recorded by a member of the household that after this interview had ended she did indeed collapse. Her health now deteriorated further, but on Tuesday 15th January she managed to take a drive in the grounds with the widowed Duchess of Coburg for company. This was to be the last time she was to leave Osborne House alive.

The state of the Queen's health got worse during the night and come the morning of 16th January she woke up feeling muddled and confused. She told her attendants that she must get up but continuously drifted off into fitful bouts of sleep. When the Royal Physician was informed he decided to visit the Queen without being summoned. He had never seen her in bed before and was rather struck by how small she appeared. It was not until after six o'clock in the evening that she finally rose and got dressed and appeared downstairs looking dazed and bewildered. It was now that Sir James Reid decided that he should

The Queen's doctor, Sir James (later Lord) Reid.   *Navy & Army Illustrated*

Sir Richard Powell Douglas MD.   *The Sphere*

warn the Royal Princesses, who were staying in the house, of the seriousness of the situation and he also to wrote to the Prince of Wales stating that the Queen showed signs of 'cerebral degeneration'. On seeing her the following day Sir James said he feared that she had suffered a mild stroke as her left cheek was drooping and her speech was showing signs of impairment.

Sir James had been observing the Queen for quite some time expecting some form of cerebal accident to occur. He secretly expected that a stroke would eventually cause the Queen's death. On seeing Her Majesty that morning he was shocked at her appearance. Her eyes were dull and staring, her skin was yellowing, she could not comprehend what was said to her and her speech was slurred and indistinct. Sometimes she knew and recognised visitors but mostly not.

Now was the time for a decision and after some thought Sir James decided that the Queen's days were numbered and so he sent for a second opinion in the person of the eminent London consultant Sir Richard Powell. The Queen agreed to this consultation, stating that Sir James must have help or the strain might prove too much for him.

Sir Richard Powell first saw Queen Victoria at eight o'clock in the evening of 17th January and he agreed with Sir James that her mind appeared to be failing. She drifted in and out of understanding and, in one of her lucid periods, enquired whether people had commented on the fact that she had not taken her usual drive. Princess Helena assured her that the weather had been so bad that no one was surprised. This, however, did not fool her mother who retorted that everyone knew that she always went out whether it rained or not. She now had periods when she was sometimes hostile and sometimes placid, whilst her skin lay in folds over her body and face.

In preparation for the final outcome Reid took the Queen's private dresser, Mrs Tuck, aside and spoke to her of the coming situation. He trained her in the techniques that he would be using and designated her the Queen's own private nurse. Sometime earlier Sir James Reid had promised the Queen that when the end was near he would tell her, but now that his honesty was required he could not bring himself to tell her.

The Prince of Wales having heard of the seriousness of his mother's illness leaves Victoria station with his sister the Duchess of Argyll for Osborne on Saturday afternoon 19th January, 1901.
London Illustrated News

The Prince of Wales, leaves Portsmouth on board the Royal Yacht *Alberta* on 19th January, 1901.
Navy & Army Illustrated

Friday 18th January seemed to be the turning point, her face sagged more, she could not swallow and she lay with her eyes shut. It was now that Sir James decided it was time to inform all the members of the Royal Family, including the Queen's grandson, the Kaiser, of the situation. The wire he sent to the Kaiser simply read 'Disquieting symptoms have developed which have caused considerable anxiety. This is private'. The Queen's son, Arthur, the Duke of Connaught, happened to be in Berlin at the time taking part in the celebrations of the 250th anniversary of the Hohenzollern dynasty. The Kaiser suggested that they should travel back to England together. During the journey to England the Kaiser insisted on driving the Imperial Train part way to Flushing and then steering his Imperial Royal Yacht across the Channel. All observers at this time remarked on the fact that he seemed happy and in high spirits and nobody could have guessed the purpose of his sudden mission.

The first official notification to the press and public that the Queen was ill was made on 18th January at six o'clock in the evening. The Prince of Wales was reluctant to make a statement for fear of causing widespread alarm and he insisted that the release be carefully worded as follows:

The Queen has not lately been in her usual health, and is unable, for the present, to take her customary drives. The Queen during the last year has had a great strain upon her powers, which has rather told on Her Majesty's nervous system. It has, therefore, been thought advisable by Her Majesty's physicians that the Queen should be kept perfectly quiet in the house and should abstain for the present from transacting business.

Word of the state of the Queen's health had spread around the Isle of Wight and soon little groups of Islanders were collecting outside the gates of Osborne House.

The whole of the household at Osborne was in a turmoil getting ready for the imminent arrival of the Royal Family wishing to be at the Queen's side. Her Majesty was totally oblivious to all this, and an observer said at the time that she seemed to spend much of the day being rather confused, although by the time the six o'clock bulletin was released she had rallied a little and managed to ask 'Have I been very ill?' The situation was now so serious that the Prince of Wales had decided that he would stay at Osborne for the duration, but he was persuaded by his sisters to return to London to try and head off the Kaiser, as it had been agreed that it would be best for the Queen if she did not know he was coming.

Here it might be useful to provide a short resumé of the children of Queen Victoria and Prince Albert :

Princess Victoria was the eldest, she was born in 1840 and died the same year as her mother. She was known as the Princess Royal and she married Prince Frederick William of Prussia. Later she became Empress Frederick and mother of the Kaiser.

Albert Edward, the Prince of Wales, was born a year later in 1841 and married Princess Alexandra of Denmark. They had five children and Bertie, as he was known in the family, acceded to the throne on his mother's death. He died in 1910.

The next child was *Princess Alice*, born in 1843 she married Louis IV the Grand Duke of Hesse-Darmstadt, they had seven children and she died in 1878.

The Prince of Wales and the Duke of York greet the Kaiser at Charing Cross on 20th January, 1901. He arrived with the Duke of Connaught at 6.30 pm and then the whole party drove to Buckingham Palace.   *London Illustrated News*

In 1844 *Prince Alfred* (Affie) was born. He was titled the Duke of Edinburgh and Saxe-Coburg-Gotha. He married the Grand Duchess Marie of Russia and they had five children. His death is dealt with elsewhere in the narrative.

Princess Helena was born in 1846 and married Prince Christian of Schleswig-Holstein. They had four children and the Princess lived until 1923.

Princess Louisa was the only one of Victoria's children not to have issue. She was born in 1848 and married the Marquis of Lorne in 1871. She died in 1939.

1850 saw the birth of *Prince Arthur*, the Duke of Connaught, who married Princess Louise of Prussia in 1879. They had three children and the Prince passed away in 1942.

Prince Leopold, the Duke of Albany, 1853-1884, married Princess Helena of Waldek-Pyrmont, who bore him three children. He died fairly young. He had haemophilia, his mother being the carrier. This was a condition prevalent in the Royal Families of Europe at this time.

The last of Victoria's children to be born and also the last to die was *Princess Beatrice* 1857-1944. She married Prince Henry of Battenberg and they had four children. One of their daughters, Victoria Eugenie (Ena) became Queen Ena of Spain. She married Don Alfonso XIII in 1906 but to do so she had to take instruction and become a convert to the Roman Catholic faith. Princess Beatrice was a constant companion of Queen Victoria during her later years and was a great comfort to her.

To continue the narrative; the situation was little changed come daybreak of Sunday 20th January but the Queen's condition deteriorated during the morning as she slipped in and out of consciousness. The Queen, in one of her lucid moments, asked whether the Prince of Wales had been informed of her condition. To make the Queen more comfortable and to assist with her nursing she was moved from her large canopied bed into a small cot and, to help her breathe, oxygen tanks were brought into the sickroom and placed at the bedside. That day was the anniversary of the death of Prince Henry of Battenberg. He was the husband of the Queen's youngest daughter Princess Beatrice and he had died serving as a British officer during the Ashanti War. A special service was held in Whippingham church at one o'clock. An half-hour earlier the Prince of Wales had left Osborne to return to London to meet the Kaiser who was due to arrive at Charing Cross station at five o'clock. During the day Sir James Reid became so alarmed with Her Majesty's now permanent semi-conscious condition that it was decided by the medical team in attendance to ask for the immediate recall of the Prince of Wales. During the day Bishop Randell Davidson, the Bishop of Winchester, had arrived and was staying with Canon Smith at Whippingham. Shortly after midnight a carriage was sent to Whippingham to summon the Bishop.

The following morning, Monday 21st January, the Queen rallied again and in fact asked for one of her favourite dogs, a white Pomeranian called Turi, which was put on the bed beside her. The Queen patted and stroked him and seemed very pleased to have him with her but the dog soon became bored and left. All this was remarkable as she had had a very bad night and nearly all hope had been given up. Quietly during the morning the Queen said to Sir James, 'I should like to live a little longer as I still have a few things to settle. I have arranged most things but there are still some left, and I want to live just a little longer'.

At 11.15 the Prince of Wales arrived with the Kaiser and they both went to the Queen's bed chamber, but as she was sleeping they both crept away. However, later the Prince managed to talk with his mother. Later that evening Sir James Reid returned to the Queen and was amazed when she grabbed his hand and kept kissing it, he concluded that she thought he was her son. For most of that night the medical team remained at the Queen's side and, when the morning of 22nd January dawned, they informed the family that in their opinion she could pass away at any moment.

A bulletin was released at eight o'clock that morning stating that: 'The Queen this morning shows signs of diminishing strength, and Her Majesty's position again assumes a more serious aspect'.

At nine o'clock the family assembled at the Queen's bedside and she looked at them and smiled. Bishop Davidson was summoned and said a few prayers and the Queen asked Princess Beatrice to summon Canon Smith to attend as well in case 'he might be hurt'.

On Sir James Reid's advice she took a little food and later the Prince of Wales asked for permission to take the Kaiser to see her. The Queen's bedroom was cleared of all the family and Sir James told her: 'Your Majesty, your grandson the Emperor is here; he has come to see you as you are so ill'.

The Queen's bedroom in the Royal Suite at Osborne was a large airy place with carefully placed pieces of furniture. The Queen did not like change in either her surroundings or her staff and here at Osborne, as at her other houses throughout the country, all the carpets, soft furnishings, drapes, curtains and covers were secretly copied without Her Majesty's knowledge so that the Queen would not notice any difference if they had to be changed for any reason. In fact, on the very rare occasions when it was thought safe to redecorate her rooms, the result had to be made to appear as though they had only been thoroughly cleaned.

The furniture in her bed chamber consisted of mahogany wardrobes and chairs, and there were also couches which were covered in the same red and green pattern chintz as in her sitting room. The salmon pink painted walls of the bed chamber were hung with many pictures, mostly those with a religious theme, the artists represented being Grissi, William Dyce, Raphael, van Eycken, Yager and Winterhalter.

The most important item of furniture in the room was the Queen's bed. It was carefully positioned to face the windows so that the Queen could look out over the countryside which she loved. The bed itself was large and very nearly square and had a heavily fringed canopy with curtains above and over it. Above the pillows was a memorial wreath, below which was a posthumous portrait of the Prince Consort. In the centre of the pillows was a bell pull and on either side a watch pocket. At the foot of the bed was a large sofa which was covered in a down quilt.

The heating came from a small fireplace which had a mantlepiece of white marble, on top of which there was a very narrow shelf on which were placed eight small busts and in the centre a carriage clock. To the right and left of the fireplace were portraits of the Prince Consort and there was also a tapestry screen.

Also within the Royal Apartments was a Prayer Room. This was a fairly simple room with a plain pulpit and altar, it also housed a small organ. Access to this room from the Queen's apartments was by a long corridor on the first floor and was created because the Queen disliked the crowds which came to stare at her when she attended Whippingham Parish Church. Once this room was opened the Queen regularly attended a service there between noon and one o'clock; she liked to be joined by those members of the Household who were available.

The Pressmen gather at the gates of Osborne to await the news of their Monarch's health.
London Illustrated News

At mid-day another bulletin was released and this stated that: 'There is no change for the worse in the Queen's condition since this morning's bulletin. The Queen has recognised the several members of the family who are here. The Queen is now asleep'.

Early in the afternoon she had another relapse and the Bishop and Canon resumed their vigil. Most of the family visited a few at a time but the Kaiser never left her side, staying kneeling for hours at her bedside and helping Sir James to move and support her when required to make her more comfortable.

Around the country preparations for the Queen's death were being made; telegraphers were ready to send the news around the world and carpenters were busy building the tiny satin-lined coffin for the Queen's small body to lie in.

The Prince of Wales now decided that a telegram to the Lord Mayor of London would help to prepare the country. The telegram read: 'My painful duty obliges me to inform you that the life of the beloved Queen is in the greatest danger'. Copies of this wire were pasted in the windows of telegraph offices all around London where crowds of people were waiting for news of the Queen's state of health.

The Queen fought to hang on to life, rallying and fading several times and at four o'clock a further bulletin was issued from Osborne House stating quite simply, 'The Queen is slowly sinking'. Shortly before the end she put out her hand towards the Prince of Wales and murmured very softly, 'Bertie'.

During the last hour of the Queen's life Bishop Davidson read her one of her favourite hymns, *Lead kindly light*. At first it did not appear that the Queen was listening but when he came to the words

> And with the morn those angel faces smile,
> Which I have loved long since and lost awhile

it was quite clear that she knew exactly what their meaning was.

Her family were gathered around to be with her and just before the end she raised herself up and gazed towards the window. There came a look of joy and recognition on her face and she said 'Oh Albert . . .', and sank down into her pillow. This naturally had a very moving effect on all those present and later Princess Helena wrote: 'I shall never forget the look of radiance on her face one felt and knew she saw beyond the Border Land - and had seen and met with all her loved ones. In death she was so beautiful, such peace and joy on her dear face - the radiance from Heaven'. The time was half past six, when the fifth female Monarch since the reign of William the Conqueror went to her maker.

When it was all over the family shook hands with Sir James Reid and the new King told him that they would never forget his services to his mother. Unfortunately not all who wished to be there arrived in time. The Prince and Princess Louis of Battenberg (the parents of Lord Louis Mountbatten) arrived at the house just after the Queen had passed away.

When Sir James Reid helped the Queen's maid lay out Her Majesty he discovered, for the first time, that she had a ventral hernia and a prolapse of the uterus. This was the first time, in the 20 years that he had been the Queen's doctor, that he had been able to examine her properly. After dinner the Prince of Wales, as he still wished to be called for the time being, asked Bishop Davidson to say a few prayers and the family all gathered in the Queen's bedroom, where she lay in white lace and with a few simple flowers around her. In her hand was put the little crucifix which she always hung over her bed. This simple act seems to contradict many things which were occurring in the religious world at that time. Only a few years previously clerics and laity were vilified for concentrating on statues and crosses.

The Lord Steward of the Royal Household in London received the following telegram soon after a quarter to seven that evening. The wire was sent by Mr Balfour, the First Lord of the Treasury, who had been waiting with a large quantity of the infamous Red Boxes for the Queen's attention. The cable read: 'The Queen died peacefully at 6.30'.

At about the same time the Prince of Wales had the following short message telegraphed to the Lord Mayor of London, a private message which was subsequently to be made public. 'My beloved mother, the Queen, has just passed away surrounded by her children and grandchildren'.

The final medical bulletin issued by Sir James Reid followed almost immediately and said much the same thing.

The Lord Mayor read the sorrowful announcement from the window of the Venetian Parlour in the Guildhall. It was heard by an enormous crowd who received the news in solemn silence. The great bell of St Paul's tolled and passing knells were rung throughout the kingdom.

In great contrast to the feelings of sorrow, loss and the hushed tones to be found within Osborne House itself, the final published bulletin was greeted with a very unseemly and undignified scramble when it was distributed to those who are euphemistically called 'the gentlemen of the press'. There had been a crowd of reporters waiting outside the gates of Osborne House for most of the day, some for several days. The final bulletin simply read 'Her Majesty breathed her last at 6.30 pm surrounded by Her Children and Grandchildren'. The moment the journalists were handed this bulletin they leapt onto bicycles, or any other form of transport that they could find, and raced away along the roads to Cowes to get their stories back to their editors as soon as possible. As they went they shouted out at the tops of their voices, 'The Queen is dead. The Queen is dead.'

The world's press was keen to hear the news, all the papers had carried reports of the Queen's illness and death and they tried to encapsulate for their readers the feelings throughout the country. They went on to describe the loss to the nation and the world and to describe how the average person in the street deeply felt the passing of this great Queen. It is often forgotten that during the Queen's long reign much of the population of the British Isles and the Empire had never known another Monarch and so this loss to them was a great tragedy. Muffled funeral bells were tolled all over the land and church services were said for the repose of her soul and to give the Royal Family comfort and support.

The Household now had to become organised and be prepared for the enormously important Lying in State period. But before this happened the household servants and the tenants were allowed up into the Queen's bedchamber to pay their last respects and to look on the old Queen just one more time. Most who saw her said that she looked so peaceful and little changed. Three hours between one o'clock and four o'clock were set aside for these people close to the Queen to file past the open coffin. However, by this time the Prince of Wales, the Duke of Connaught, the Duke of York, Prince Christian and the Duke of Argyll had left for London to attend a meeting of the Privy Council. Later that day, after the meeting, the Prince of Wales was proclaimed King by the Great Officers of State and High Ranking Officers of the Royal Household.

The following day most of the Royal Family were back at Osborne House, where the dining room had been prepared as a chapel and a company of the Rifle Reserve stood guard over the room. Soon after taking breakfast Sir James Reid took charge of preparing the Queen's coffin after the nature of her very detailed instructions divulged only to him. Then Sir James, with the assistance of the King, the Kaiser and the Duke of Connaught lifted her body into the coffin after it had been wrapped in her wedding veil.

The Queen had left notice with Sir James that she wanted several of her treasured possessions buried with her. Quietly over the last few days the doctor and Mrs Tuck had collected together the mementos that Victoria had specified. Into the bottom of the coffin they put jewels, pictures, photographs and small statues and laid alongside the Queen were a plaster cast of the Prince Consort's hand and the dressing gown Princess Alice had embroidered for him. It is then that a secret and intimate moment occurred. The Royal Family withdrew and Sir James, following the Queen's private instructions, placed a small tissue wrapped package containing a photograph of John Brown and a lock of his hair in her left hand, and before the mourners returned to pay their last respects, he had tactfully covered the photograph with a floral display and covered her face with her wedding veil. The Order of the Garter was also placed over her chest.

The King knowing his mother's affection for her Indian servant the Munshi Abdul Karim, who entered Royal Service after the death of John Brown, sent a personal invitation to him to come into the Queen's bedchamber and pay his last respects.

The tenants of the Osborne estate file slowly past the coffin while it lies in Osborne House.
The Sphere

This indication of concern did not last long, because as soon as it was possible the King had the Munshi sent home. When all was done the coffin was closed and the lid was secured. During the following morning, 25th January, a party of Blue Jackets carefully carried it down the stairs and into the hastily prepared temporary chapel.

When the body was brought down all the members of the Royal Household stood at the bottom of the stairs to witness its passing. The King and the Emperor and the other gentlemen from the Royal Family followed the coffin in procession into the room where it was laid on a bier which was covered with the Royal Standard. After all had assembled a short service was held in the presence of all the Royal Family. A company of the Grenadier Guards had been summoned from London and they guarded the body of the late Queen during the Lying in State in the chapel until it left the House on its final journey. The Kaiser was much moved and later stated that one of his most treasured possessions was the Union Flag which had been draped over his grandmother's coffin.

The next two days were busy not only for those arranging the details of the funeral, details which the Queen herself had left because, as she had said many times, 'I love funerals', but for the staff and household of the House. Sunday, 26th January was a wild and windy day and it was also the Kaiser's birthday and a great many people arrived at Osborne House to offer their birthday greetings. At 8.45 all the old Queen's Household and the new King's Household, representatives from the German Embassy and the officers of His Imperial Yacht were assembled in the Council Room for this purpose. Later the whole family present went to Divine Service at Whippingham, where the Bishop of Winchester preached.

The Duke and Duchess of Connaught left Osborne on the 28th January and went up to London for the night. Meanwhile an investiture was held. This was the Investiture into the Order of the Garter of the Crown Prince of Germany. Most of the Royal Family were present as were the Duke of Norfolk and the Bishop of Winchester, who was there as Prelate of the Order of the Garter.

The next day dawned bright but cold and the King had to leave the Isle of Wight to travel to London to receive officially the loyal addresses from the House of Lords and the House of Commons. Meanwhile several of the late Queen's attendants from London arrived at Osborne to view the Lying in State. Osborne House at this time saw the comings and goings of many people. To add to the complications within the Household the Duke of York developed German measles. On the Wednesday, in the early afternoon, 12 of the members of the Royal Family left, these were mainly the younger members, and at a quarter to five the King returned from London.

The Bishop of Winchester.
London Illustrated News

The funeral cortège leaves Osborne
House *en route* to Cowes.
Author's Collection

The Queen leaves Osborne House for
the last time.   *Author's Collection*

Chapter Two

The Journey Begins

Since the death of the Queen, and most probably for quite some time beforehand, plans were being made to conduct her last journey with all the dignity and decorum that befitted a great Monarch. During her lifetime Her Majesty was always very interested in the ceremonies and rituals surrounding death and funerals and over the years she had compiled very detailed instructions for her own funeral. This Royal Funeral had to be correct. It had to be an occasion which would be fitting for a great Queen, known by some as the grandmother of Europe because of all her family connections, and the daughter of a distinguished soldier. In other words, a full ceremonial military state funeral. Among some of the instructions the Queen had left were notes which she had made several years earlier after she had spoken to Alfred, Lord Tennyson. The poet, who also loved the Isle of Wight, had convinced her that white should be the colour of a funeral, a celebration of life, not black, a sign of death, and instructions that white and purple were to be the dominant colours of all the drapes and trappings in all areas were relayed to those making and organising the arrangements.

After transporting the Prince of Wales back to the Island the smaller of the Royal Yachts, the *Alberta*, had for some time been moored at Cowes in preparation for the beginning of the last journey. During the morning of Friday 1st February, 1901 the coffin was taken from Osborne House, still under guard and accompanied by pipers, through the lanes of the Island and the streets of Cowes and was solemnly embarked onto the *Alberta* at Trinity Pier on the River Medina. The *Alberta* was built in 1863 in Pembroke Dock. She was a wooden-hulled paddle steamer 160 ft in length with a displacement of 320 tons and was built as a tender to the larger Royal Yacht, the *Victoria and Albert*. When all was secured, and at a signal from the King, the yacht sailed. It was just after three o'clock on a bright, clear afternoon. Four floral emblems had been placed at the four corners of the coffin while it crossed to the mainland. They were in the form of four anchors of white lilies, azaleas and lilies-of-the-valley, with ropes of violets. These tributes came from the four naval commands, the Nore, Devonport, Portsmouth and the Channel Squadron.

Once the *Alberta* left, under the command of the Aides-de-Camp Capt. May and Capt. Poe, the King boarded the other, much larger, Royal Yacht, the *Victoria and Albert*. She had been built in 1899 and was screw driven with a displacement of 5,500 tons. The Kaiser boarded his own Imperial Yacht and members of the Government followed aboard the *Scott*. The four vessels then proceeded across the Solent in line astern.

The tiny yacht carrying the coffin across from the Island was dwarfed by the two rows of naval warships which had been drawn up to provide a Guard of Honour from Cowes to Portsmouth Harbour. From mid-day onward 80 one minute guns were fired, the first salvo being fired by HMS *Australia*. The warships were not only British vessels, there were also some from other nations

Above: Members of many Royal families followed the gun carriage as it passed through the streets on its way to Cowes.

Right: An engraving showing sailors carrying the coffin on board the *Alberta* while it was moored up at the Trinity Pier in Cowes.

including the *Hatsuse* which had been sent by the Mikado. Here lies an irony, the fact that the Mikado should send a ship to honour the late Queen, a woman who was inordinately fond of the Savoy operettas of W.S. Gilbert and Sir Arthur Sullivan. *The Mikado* was one of her particular favourites.

It was later reported that the minute guns could be heard as far away as Beachy Head and Tunbridge Wells, probably due to the unusually still atmosphere and cold air. Similar guns were also being fired in Melbourne and the Cape and everywhere throughout the Colonies intense grief was felt.

The sad procession slipped slowly through the mouth of Portsmouth harbour and passed under the shadow of Nelson's great flagship HMS *Victory*, as the sound of Chopin's 'Funeral March' wafted across the water. The *Alberta* moored at the Royal Clarence Yard in Gosport at 4.40 pm, whilst the *Victoria and Albert* and another of the Royal Yachts, the *Osborne*, with other members of the Royal Family aboard, moored in the harbour. The German Imperial Yacht berthed at the Southern Jetty of Portsmouth Dockyard.

Once the *Alberta* was alongside, two guards of honour were stationed at the pier, one consisting of 200 seamen from HMS *Excellent* and the other a detachment of 400 Royal Marines. At this time naval pensioners were employed in the Royal Clarence Yard and they also were deployed in the guard of honour. During the night a detachment of 32 marines guarded where the body lay and a series of picket boats patrolled the waters of the harbour.

This was a day when all flags were flown at half-mast and the passage was witnessed by many thousands of ordinary people. Later a report in one of the local papers stated that the whole event was conducted in brilliant sunshine. The words lodged in the official records of the City of Portsmouth state that:

> Portsmouth witnessed the passing of a great Queen. In brilliant weather, the coffin containing the body of Queen Victoria was borne across the Solent passing a long line of British and foreign warships, which fired minute guns, the shore batteries continuing the mournful salute until the Yacht arrived at Clarence Yard, whence the body was taken to London by rail the next morning.

Looking at other reports and tracts from the period, this report seems to be very accurate. The coffin was laid in the station wating room under guard, and the funeral carriage was taken to a spot behind the Guard House of St George Barracks.

The train was guarded by sentries, the crossing gates were closed behind it and the massive wooden doors on the tunnel through the ramparts closed in front of it locking it into a secure position to stay overnight.

Once the preparations for the Royal Funeral were well underway the members of the Queen's Royal Household, Ladies-in-Waiting, dressers and ladies' maids, along with other travelling members of the Household, left Osborne House as the Court transferred back to London. The new King would not be returning to Osborne House time and again, as his mother had done, he did not have her affection for the Isle of Wight. The Queen had spent her early married life there and the memories must have been legion. Many of the retinue who travelled at this time knew that this was to be the last time that they would see Osborne House as a Royal residence.

Left: The Royal Yacht *Alberta* leaves Cowes on its way into Portsmouth Harbour to berth near the Royal Clarence Yard in Gosport.
Author's Collection

Above: Royal Yacht *Alberta* passes through the ships drawn up in the Solent as she steams past with the body of the Late Queen aboard.
Author's Collection

Right: The *Alberta* sails in through the harbour mouth at Portsmouth with its sad cargo. She was followed in by the *Victoria and Albert.*
Author's Collection

The Royal Yacht *Victoria and Albert*.   *Author's Collection*

Crew of the *Victoria and Albert*.   *Author's Collection*

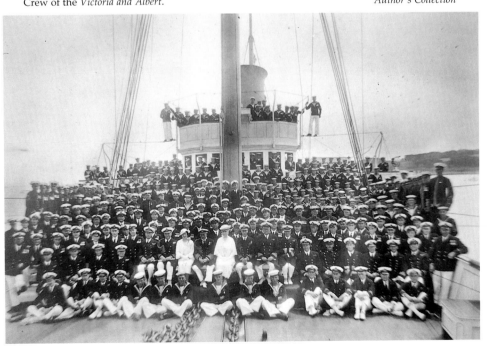

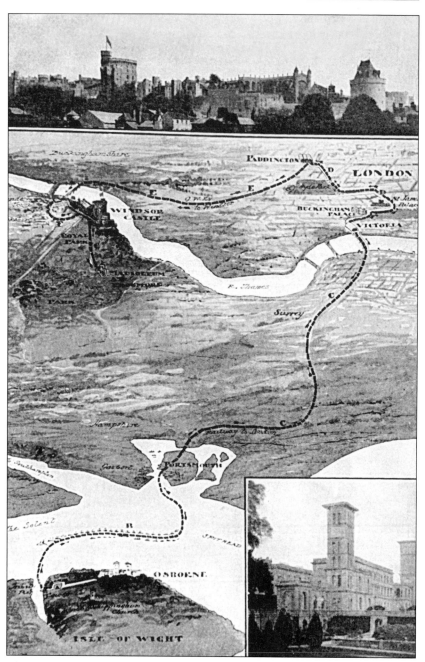

The funeral route as printed in *The Sphere*. The sharp eyed will notice that the train is shown travelling via Portsmouth, when in actual fact it left from Gosport.   *The Sphere*

The retinue were moved by ferry boat and yacht from both Ryde and Cowes but it is reasonable to assume that the heavy Royal luggage, trucks and bags, etc. travelled across from the Island via the same route. This route would have been from Ryde to Stokes Bay Pier in Gosport where the luggage was unloaded and placed into railway vans for transportation to London and beyond.

Once the *Victoria and Albert* had arrived in Portsmouth Harbour the King sent for the yacht carpenters, who had constructed the catafalque on which the coffin had lain, and the Petty Officers who had acted as bearers. The men were paraded before the King and in front of the Royal Saloon and His Majesty told them that they had been employed on a very grave and solemn duty which they had performed remarkably well. The Queen, he said, had instituted the Victorian Medal a few years earlier and he was bestowing this medal on them, not for his own sake, but for the sake of his late beloved mother whom they had faithfully served for many years.

The logistics of moving the Royal Train across the railway system was another interesting problem. The actual movement from Gosport to Windsor had to be meticulously planned and the Chairmen of the three railway companies, the London & South Western, the London, Brighton & South Coast, and the Great Western, which were all to be involved, had discussions long into the night. Plans were made, submitted and rejected. The final decision on the route of the Royal Train was to be made by the new King.

The railway companies all wanted to be represented at the funeral and eventually the London, Brighton & South Coast Railway (LB&SCR) Royal Train was commissioned for this part of the journey, to which a Great Western Saloon was added to carry the coffin itself. The LB&SCR Royal Train had travelled to Portsmouth on 23rd January and carried King Edward VII on his return journey to the Isle of Wight after the Privy Council meeting where he had been officially proclaimed King.

Everything had to be right for the day, the Royal Train had returned empty to Brighton after the King had alighted but it returned again in the next few days for test purposes, making an experimental run onto the South railway jetty line to test clearances. At this time there had been some talk of landing the body there within the Portsmouth Dockyard. It is well known how the Queen disliked Portsmouth, so it would have been strange if this plan had been adopted.

The final itinerary for the train was not decided until late on 31st January, after the King had personally selected and verified the route. A point of some interest is the selection of the LB&SCR route to Victoria via Havant, for it was well known that the late Queen had no love for that company. Maybe because it had the word Brighton in the name and she believed that she had been treated discourteously there in the early years of her reign. Yet another one of those towns not favoured by the late Queen.

The royal remains were to be conveyed on a specially constructed bier which was draped entirely in purple and fixed in the centre of the Great Western First Class Saloon No. 229. Things had to be altered and the existing drapes in the carriage, in accordance with the late Queen's wishes, were changed to purple and white and were hung alternately round the interior walls of the coach, the material used was velvet. The windows were covered

Drawing of Royal Victoria station in Royal Clarence Yard in the 1890s.
Gosport Railway Society

A sketch map showing the location of the Royal Victoria station within Royal Clarence Yard, and the route the Funeral Train took to reach Fareham.
Gosport Railway Society

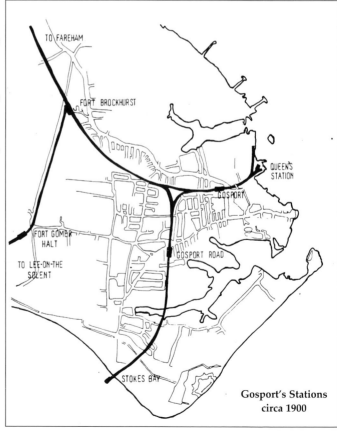

Gosport's Stations circa 1900

Queen Victoria's Landing stage 1901.
Gosport Railway Society

Royal Clarence Yard Pier 1901.
Gosport Railway Society

Royal Clarence Yard Pier (George Leaf Lantern Slide). *Gosport Railway Society*

Royal Victoria station in Royal Clarence Yard in 1901.   *Gosport Railway Society*

Royal Clarence Yard (from a George Leaf Lantern Slide), 1901.   *Gosport Railway Society*

Two aerial views of Royal Clarence Yard in 1966.   *(Both) Gosport Railway Society*

Architectural plan of Royal Victoria station.
Gosport Railway Society

L & S.W.R

Royal Clarence Yard Gosport

The Queen's Private Station.

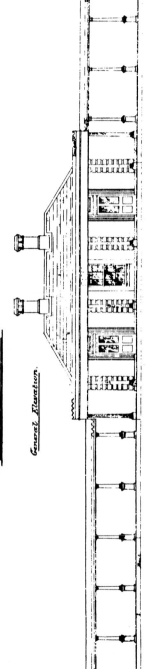

General Elevation.

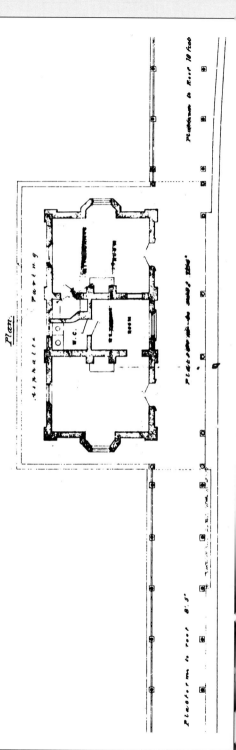

Plan.

Platform to Roof 10 feet.

Platform to Roof 8.5'

Notice behind the Guard House of St George Barracks.   *Gosport Railway Society*

Interior of Royal Victoria station in Royal Clarence Yard, Gosport in 1965.

Gosport Railway Society

LONDON & SOUTH WESTERN RAILWAY.

SPECIAL NOTICE No. 136, 1901.

INSTRUCTIONS TO STATION MASTERS, INSPECTORS, ENGINEMEN, GUARDS, SIGNALMEN, PLATELAYERS, GATEMEN, AND ALL CONCERNED

AS TO

A SPECIAL TRAIN,

CONVEYING THE BODY OF HER LATE MAJESTY

QUEEN VICTORIA

HIS MAJESTY KING EDWARD VII.,

HIS IMPERIAL MAJESTY THE GERMAN EMPEROR

AND OTHER ROYAL PERSONAGES

FROM

THE ROYAL CLARENCE YARD, GOSPORT, TO HAVANT JUNC.,

En route to

VICTORIA STATION (L. B. & S. C. RLY.)
ON SATURDAY, 2ND FEBRUARY.

ROYAL CLARENCE YARD to HAVANT JUNCTION en route to VICTORIA.

	L. & S.W. Co.'s Pilot Engine.		L.B. & S.C. Co.'s Pilot Engine.		Royal Train.		
	ARR.	DEP.	ARR.	DEP.	ARR.	DEP.	
	A.M.	A.M.	A.M.	A.M.	A.M.	A.M.	
Royal Clarence Yard	...	8 35	...	...	...	8 45	
Gosport	8 38		...	...	...	8 48	The 8.40 a.m. Train Portsmouth Harbour to Southampton to be held back at Portcreek Junction until the Royal Train has passed Cosham Junction.
Fort Brockhurst							
Fareham	...	8 44	...	8 48	8 54	8 58 B	
Botley	8 55				...	...	A.—Set down L.& S.W. Co.'s Pilotmen.
Cosham	...	...	8 57		9 7		
Cosham Junction	...	...	8 58		9 8	The Royal Train will not stop to set down Pilotmen.
Farlington Junction	...	...	9 0		9 10		
Havant	...	...	9A3½		9 13½	B.—Change Engines.
Havant Junction	...	...	9 4		9 14		
Victoria (L.B. & S.C. Ry.)		10 50	...	11 0			

Sub-Inspector Langdown to travel on the Pilot Engine between Royal Clarence Yard and Havant. Inspector Elliott to be at Fareham. Chief Inspector Greenfield in charge of the Train, as between Royal Clarence Yard and Havant, assisted by Chief Inspector Ottaway.

No Train or Engine must be allowed to pass the Royal Train on the opposite line of rails.

Special Traffic Notice issued by the LSWR.

Private and not for Publication.	SUPPLEMENT to SPECIAL NOTICE No. 6.

LONDON AND SOUTH WESTERN RAILWAY
AND
LONDON BRIGHTON AND SOUTH COAST RAILWAY.

Station Masters and Heads of Departments must see that a copy of this Notice is handed to every person who may be in any way engaged in connection with the working of the Train, including Signalmen, Crossing Keepers, Flagmen and Porgmen, who must read it carefully, and strictly not say to and obey the instructions contained therein. No excuse at knowledge of these instructions can be accepted as an excuse for any failure or neglect of duty.

TO THE OFFICERS AND SERVANTS OF THIS AND OTHER COMPANIES CONCERNED.

FUNERAL TRAIN CONVEYING THE

BODY OF HER LATE MAJESTY QUEEN VICTORIA,
Accompanied by the Chief Mourner,

H.M. KING EDWARD VII.
AND
H.I.M. THE GERMAN EMPEROR
AND THE OTHER ROYAL PRINCES,

On SATURDAY, FEBRUARY 2nd, 1901.

FROM GOSPORT (S.W.R.) TO VICTORIA *(via Fareham, Cosham, Havant, Ford Junction, Horsham, Dorking and Mitcham Junction):—*

TIME TABLE.

	PILOT.	ROYAL TRAIN.		PILOT.	ROYAL TRAIN.
	A.M.	A.M.		A.M.	A.M.
UP JOURNEY.	arr. | dep.	arr. | dep.	UP JOURNEY.	arr. | dep.	arr. | dep.
Gosport (Clarence Yard, S.W.R.)	... 8 35	... 8 45	Stammerham Junction	9 32	10 3
Gosport	8 38	8 48	Horsham	9 35	10 5
Fareham	8 44	8 54 8 56	Warnham	9 44	10 8
Cosham	8 57	9 7	Ockley	10 3	10 12
Farlington Junction	9 0	9 10	Holmwood	10 6	10 16
Havant Junction	9 5	9 15	Dorking	10 13	10 23
Bosham	9 11	9 21	Leatherhead Junction	10 18	10 28
Chichester	9 15	9 25	Epsom Junction	10 23	10 33
Drayton	9 17	9 27	Sutton Junction	10 28	10 38
Barnham Junction	9 22	9 32	Mitcham Junction	10 33	10 43
Ford Junction	9 26	9 36	Streatham Junction South	10 37	10 47
Arundel	9 30	9 40	Balham Junction (Main Line)	10 40	10 50
Amberley	9 34	9 44	Clapham Junction	10 44	10 54
Hardham Junction	9 39	9 49	Grosvenor Road (slowly)	10 48	10 52
Pulborough	9 40	9 50	Victoria	10 50 ...	11 0 ...
Billingshurst	9 46	9 56			

The Royal Train will consist of eight Vehicles.
On leaving Fareham, the Vehicles forming the Royal Train will run in the following order, viz. :—
Brake Van, Saloon, Funeral Car, Royal Saloon, Saloon, Bogie First and Brake Van.
The Pilot Engine and the Engine of the Royal Train will carry the following Head Signals.
Clear Weather :— Three White Boards with a Double Diamond painted on them, one on top of Smoke Box and one on each end of Buffer Beam.
Foggy Weather :— Four Lights. A Green Light on top of Smoke Box, a Green Light on centre of Buffer Beam, and a White Light on each end of Buffer Beam.

South Western Company's Engines and Guards will work the above Services from Gosport to Fareham.
Brighton Company's Engines and Guards will work forward from Fareham (S.W.R.) to Victoria, the Pilot and Royal Train being in charge of South Western Company's Pilotmen from Fareham (S.W.R.) to Farlington Junction.

Instructions for working Queen Victoria's funeral train issued jointly by the LSWR and LB&SCR.

SHUNTINGS FOR THE ROYAL SPECIAL TRAIN.

To avoid all chance of detention every Engine, Train or Vehicle must be cleared off and not allowed to proceed upon or cross the Main Line at any part between Gosport and Victoria for at least Twenty Minutes before the Royal Special Train is due as per Time Table on other side.

9.0 a.m. Portsmouth Town to Brighton to follow the Royal Train from Farlington Junction.

8.45 a.m. Portsmouth Harbour to London Bridge to leave at 8.35 a.m., shunt at Chichester and follow the Royal Train from that Station.

9.38 a.m. Ford to Arundel to follow the Royal Train from Ford Junction.

8.45 a.m. Chichester to London, via Midhurst, to follow the Royal Train from Hardham Junction.

9.6 a.m. Ford Junction to Pulborough to run punctually so as not to delay the Pilot Engine and the Royal Train.

7.56 a.m Portsmouth Harbour to London Bridge to pass Streatham Junction South not later than 10.27 a.m., but if running late to shunt at Epsom and follow the Royal Train from that Station.

S. W. R. Co.'s 10.15 a.m. Leatherhead to Epsom to follow the Royal Train from Leatherhead Junction.

INSTRUCTIONS FOR WORKING ROYAL TRAINS.

(TO BE KEPT STRICTLY PRIVATE.)

PRELIMINARY PRECAUTIONS TO BE OBSERVED.

1. All Signal Boxes on the route both at Stations and at intermediate Block Posts which in the ordinary course would be closed, must be opened and the signals lighted when necessary at least one hour before the "Pilot" is due, and must remain so until the Royal Train has been signalled clear from the Block Post in advance

2. The Line must be kept clear 20 Minutes before the Royal Special Train is due, as shown on the accompanying Time Table, and no Train, Engine or Vehicle (except the "Pilot" Engine) must be allowed to proceed upon, cross, or foul the running Line from Gosport to Fareham, Fareham to Farlington, or the Up Main Line from Farlington to Victoria within this interval.

3. Goods Trains must not be allowed to leave any Station on the Line on which the Royal Train will run unless they can reach the next Station at which they can be shunted out of the way at least 20 Minutes before the Pilot Engine and 30 Minutes before the Royal Train will be due at that Station.

4. All Shunting operations on the Lines or Sidings adjoining the Line on which the Royal Train will run, must be suspended at least 30 minutes before the Royal Train is due, and not be resumed until after it has passed.

5. Arrangements must also be made for the Shunting or Stopping of Goods, Mineral or Cattle Trains running over the next adjacent running Line or Lines, so that no Train, with the exception of Passenger Trains, may be allowed to travel on those Lines between any two adjacent Stations within 15 minutes of the Royal Train being due to pass. The Trains must be brought to a stand at the last Station where they can call, and remain under the protection of Signals in compliance with this order; the Guards of such Trains will be held responsible (under the Station Masters) for carefully examining the loading of the Trucks in their Trains directly they come to a stand, to see that nothing is projecting.

6. Drivers of Trains standing in Sidings or adjoining Lines, waiting for the passing of the Royal Train, must prevent their Engines emitting Smoke, or making a noise by blowing off Steam, or Whistling when the Royal Train is passing. In like manner, the Engines of Passenger Trains passing the Royal Train on adjoining Lines must avoid Whistling or blowing off Steam when passing, unless absolutely necessary.

7. Station Masters must previously arrange for reliable men to be placed at Facing Points (over which the Royal Train will run) 30 minutes before the Royal Train is due, and remain there until it has passed. They must also arrange for such Facing Points to be carefully examined and securely clipped and padlocked for the Line over which the Royal Train will pass, shortly before the passing of the Pilot. After the Royal Train has passed, the clip and padlock must be withdrawn, and kept carefully in the Signal Box until they are again required. Station Masters are also required to visit each Signal Box connected with their Stations, and satisfy themselves that each Signalman and the other Staff concerned are thoroughly acquainted with the arrangements for the Royal Train, and that the Flagmen and others required for special duties are properly posted, and thoroughly understand what is required of them, and are duly supplied with the necessary Hand Signals and Detonators.

8. Every precaution must be used, and a strict watch kept to prevent any work going on at the various Stations, which might in any way affect the Line on which the Royal Train will run. The greatest vigilance must be observed at, and adjacent to, all Stations through which the Royal Train will pass.

9. The Station Masters at Stations where there is not a separate Goods Staff, and the Goods Agents at the Stations where the Goods Yard is under the control of the Agent, must go round the Sidings adjacent to the Line upon which the Royal Train is running, and satisfy themselves personally, 30 minutes before the Royal Train is due, that everything is well clear of that Line, and is kept so until the Royal Train has passed.

10. Station Masters must personally see that all approach road Gates (except those which Passengers may have to pass through), and Gates leading to Goods Yards and Sidings, are closed and locked 30 minutes before the Royal Train is due. The keys must afterwards remain in their possession until after the Royal Train has passed.

11. Station Masters must personally see that all junctions and entrances to the Stations are watched and kept quite clear and private. Where necessary, Station Masters and Goods Agents must act in concert for the purpose of carrying out the foregoing arrangements.

FOGMEN'S DUTIES.

12. The Fogmen must have special instructions to be at their posts 30 minutes before the Royal Train is due, whether the weather is foggy or not, and they must remain there until after the Royal Train has passed. If there is a fog they must take care that the detonators which are placed on the rails after the passage of the Pilot Engine, are taken up again immediately the Signals are lowered for the Royal Train to pass.

PILOT ENGINE AND ROYAL TRAIN.

13. No Engine, Train or Vehicle must be allowed to be upon or cross the Line on which the Royal Train will run after the passing of the "Pilot," until the Royal Train has passed.

2

Instructions for working Queen Victoria's funeral train issued jointly by the LSWR and LB&SCR.

INSTRUCTIONS FOR WORKING ROYAL TRAINS—*continued.*

EQUIPMENT OF ROYAL TRAIN.

14. The Royal Train is furnished with the Westinghouse Continuous Brake, which must be worked in strict accordance with the Instructions issued on the subject.

EXAMINERS.

15. Examiners to accompany the Royal Train throughout the Journey, in order to render assistance, if necessary; but they must not touch the Train unless required to do so.

GUARDS.

16. The Head Guard must enter in his report the number of persons who travel by the Royal Train [other than the Railway Officials] and also particulars of any animals that may be conveyed in the Train. The Front Guard must keep his face towards the rear of the Train and be constantly on the look-out to observe any signal that may be given by any of the Guards or other attendants accompanying the Royal Train, and must communicate instantly to the Driver any Signal he may receive.

EMERGENCY TELEGRAPH INSTRUMENT.

17. A Telegraph Instrument with the necessary Appliances will be conveyed by the Royal Train, by means of which Telegraphic communication can at once be established at any place in case of need ; the call for this special service will be " R L." To this Signal precedence must be given. Competent telegraph men, under the charge of the Telegraph Superintendent, will accompany the Train.

INSTRUCTIONS AS TO REDUCTION OF SPEED AT CERTAIN POINTS.

18. Any · instructions which may be in force with respect to slackening speed owing to New Works, Relaying Operations, Junctions, &c., applicable to the route over which the Train will run, must be strictly observed.

19. Detonators must be used for the Royal Train only in cases of emergency, and during Fogs or falling Snow, but must not be used to call attention to the ordinary relaying operations or other works of which a written or printed Notice has been issued, stating that Trains are to run at reduced speed over those portions of the Line where such works are in progress.

20. In order that there may be no misunderstanding, the Enginemen of the Pilot Engine, and of the Royal Train, before they commence the journey, must be supplied with all such notices relating to the Line over which the Royal Train has to run, and the Locomotive Superintendents, before starting, must fully explain to them the instructions, and make them clearly understand between what points the Pilot Engine and Royal Train must run at the reduced speeds mentioned in the notices.

PLATELAYERS TO SIGNAL ROYAL TRAIN.

21. The Engineering Department will provide Platelayers to be stationed along the Line, in good time before the " Pilot " is due, within signalling distance of each other, to signal the Royal Train.

22. Station Masters at the various Stations must provide themselves with Detonators and Hand-Signals, and supply the same to Platelayers as required for this special purpose. Station Masters will be held responsible for collecting them again after the Royal Train has run. The Gangers are responsible for fully instructing the Platelayers.

23. If all is right for the Royal Train to proceed, the Platelayers must exhibit a Green Hand-Signal held steadily in the hand ; if they wish to caution the Driver to reduce speed, a Green Hand-Signal must be waved from side to side ; and if it should be necessary to stop the Train, three Detonators must be placed on the rails and a Red Hand-Signal exhibited.

LEVEL CROSSINGS.

24. At all Level Crossings at which Gatemen are stationed, the men in charge must be on duty ; and at all Level or Occupation Crossings at which no men are regularly stationed, Platelayers, provided with Hand Signals and Detonators, must be placed in charge 45 minutes before the " Pilot " is due to pass, and they must satisfy themselves that there is no obstruction, and must remain at their posts until 10 minutes after the Royal Train has passed. The Gangers will be responsible for seeing that this is done, and will receive their instructions from the District Inspectors of Permanent Way. Nothing must be allowed to cross the Line at any Level or Occupation Crossing 15 minutes before the Pilot Engine is due to pass, and under no circumstances must anything be allowed to cross the Line at any Crossing after the Pilot Engine has passed until the Royal Train has passed.

STARTING THE ROYAL TRAIN.

25. The Signal for starting the Train must be given by the Guards in strict accordance with Rule 171, in the Book of Regulations, and care must be taken that the Royal Personages, and all the members of the Suite, are seated before the Signal is given.

The Signal must not be given before the Guard has been verbally informed by the Foreman in charge of the Examiners that their examination of the Train has been completed.

SIGNALLING THE PILOT AND THE ROYAL TRAIN.

26. Immediately after the Pilot Engine has passed, the word " Pilot " must be telegraphed to the next Box in Circuit. Immediately after the " Warning " Signal for the Royal Train has been given, the word " Royal " must be telegraphed to the next Box in Circuit.

27. Not until the Pilot Engine has passed the Starting Signal, and is proceeding, or has been shunted clear of the line on which the Royal Train will run, must the " Line Clear " Signal be given to the Station in the rear.

28. If the " Line Clear " Signal has not been given by the Box in advance for the Pilot Engine, the Royal Train must be stopped, in accordance with the Block Regulations.

29. No Signalman must give permission for the Train which next follows the Royal Train to leave the Station in rear until the " Line Clear " Signal has been received for the Royal Train from the Station in advance ; and at Stations where two or more Signal Boxes exist a short distance apart, the Royal Train must have passed through the Station and into the outside section beyond, before any following Train is allowed to enter the Station.

30. A constant watch is to be kept on the Telegraph Instruments during the time the Pilot Engine and the Royal Train are running between the Stations on either side, Up and Down. Where a Telegraph Clerk is not kept the Station Master must watch the Instrument himself, except at the time when he is watching the passage of the Pilot and the Royal Train, as shewn in clause 33.

3

Instructions for working Queen Victoria's funeral train issued jointly by the LSWR and LB&SCR.

INSTRUCTIONS FOR WORKING ROYAL TRAINS—*continued.*

PILOT ENGINES.

31. Pilot Engines will stand at the following Stations :—Chichester, Ford Junction, Horsham, Epsom After the Royal Train has passed Ford Junction, the Station Master at Ford Junction to advise Chichester to return the Pilot Engine to Portsmouth.

After the Royal Train has passed Horsham, the Station Master at Horsham to advise Ford Junction to return the Pilot Engine to Brighton.

After the Royal Train has passed Epsom, the Station Master at Epsom to advise Horsham to return the Pilot Engine to Brighton.

After the Royal Train has passed Mitcham Junction, the Station Master at Mitcham Junction to advise Epsom to return the Pilot Engine to New Cross.

STATIONS TO BE KEPT CLEAR AND PRIVATE.

32. *All the Stations must be kept perfectly clear and private during the passage of the Royal Train, and no persons (excepting those properly authorised, Passengers travelling in the opposite direction, the Company's Servants on duty, and the Police at those Stations where their services are required) are to be admitted to any of the Stations on the route. The Servants of the Company are to perform the necessary work on the Platforms without noise, and no cheering or other demonstration must be allowed, the object being that the Royal Party shall be perfectly undisturbed during the journey, all the Stations being kept perfectly clear and private.*

33. The Station Masters must be on duty to watch the passage of the Pilot Engine and also the Royal Train.

TERMINATION OF ROYAL JOURNEY.

34. At any platform at which His Majesty has to alight, a distinctive chalk mark must be made at the exact spot at which the Footplate of the Engine should be when the Train stops, and a man with a Red Flag must stand on the Platform at the chalk mark to ensure the Train being stopped dead at the appointed place.

INFORMATION TO BE KEPT PRIVATE.

35. Under no circumstances is information to be given to any person (other than those who must necessarily be made acquainted with the arrangements) respecting the time of the running of the Royal Train, or any other circumstances connected therewith. Platelayers and all other men concerned must be strictly enjoined not to give any information to any one not concerned with the running of the Royal Train.

The Royal Train must be telegraphed as follows :—

36. The Station Masters at the starting and destination Stations must wire the General Manager and the Superintendent of the Line immediately, and state the exact time at which the Royal Train started or arrived, as the case may be.

37. Station Masters are requested to see that the Telegraph Clerks are at their instruments two hours before the Royal Train is due to leave the Terminal Station, and that they do not go away on any pretence whatever.

38. The time of departure or passing of the Royal Train must be telegraphed on the Speaking Instruments with the RTM. prefix in the following manner, and in the order set forth below, in addition to the proper signalling on the Block Signalling Instruments :—" *Royal Train passed (or left)*." [*Here give the time.*]

UP JOURNEY.	UP JOURNEY.
FAREHAM (S.W.R.) TO TELEGRAPH Cosham, Farlington Junction, Havant, Emsworth, Bosham and Chichester.	PULBOROUGH TO TELEGRAPH Horsham, Warnham, Ockley, Holmwood and Dorking.
HAVANT TO TELEGRAPH Chichester, Drayton, Barnham Junction, Ford Junction, Horsham and Victoria. *Ford Junction Station must immediately transmit this message to Ford Junction Box and Arundel Junction on the Signal Box Circuit.*	HORSHAM TO TELEGRAPH Dorking, Box Hill, Leatherhead, Epsom and Victoria. *Leatherhead must immediately inform the Junction Signalman, also transmit the message to Ashtead and Epsom Junction (L. & S.W. Railway).*
CHICHESTER TO TELEGRAPH Ford Junction, Amberley, Arundel and Pulborough. *Pulborough must immediately transmit this message to Hardham Junction on the Signal Box Circuit.*	DORKING TO TELEGRAPH Epsom, Sutton and Mitcham Junction. *Mitcham Junction must immediately transmit this message to Streatham Junction South on the Signal Box Circuit.*
FORD JUNCTION TO TELEGRAPH Pulborough, Billingshurst and Horsham. *Horsham must immediately transmit this message to Stammerham Junction and Itchingfield Junction on the Signal Box Circuit.*	EPSOM TO TELEGRAPH Mitcham Junction, Balham, Clapham Junction and Victoria.
	MITCHAM JUNCTION TO TELEGRAPH Clapham Junction, Battersea Park, Grosvenor Road and Victoria.
	BALHAM TO TELEGRAPH Victoria.

39. Immediately on receipt of these Telegrams, each Station Master must forward the information to all the Signal Boxes under his control.

40. Copies of these Telegrams, showing the times received and forwarded, and full particulars of any delay, must be sent the same day to the Electrical Superintendent, London Bridge.

☞ *The receipt of these Special Traffic Notices to be acknowledged on the Form sent herewith, which must be returned by first Train.*

<table>
<tr><td style="text-align:center">CHAS. J. OWENS,
General Manager (L. & S.W.R.).
SAM FAY,
Superintendent of the Line (L. & S.W.R.).</td><td style="text-align:center">WILLIAM FORBES,
General Manager (L.B. & S.C.R.).
D. GREENWOOD,
Superintendent of the Line (L.B. & S.C.R.).</td></tr>
</table>

OFFICE OF SUPERINTENDENT OF THE LINE,
LONDON BRIDGE STATION,
(2,100)   *February 1st, 1901.*

WATERLOW & SONS LIMITED, PRINTERS, LONDON WALL, LONDON.

Instructions for working Queen Victoria's funeral train issued jointly by the LSWR and LB&SCR.

and the only light came from six gas lamps fixed in the clerestory roof and the exterior of the carriage was repainted.

All the stations on the route were cleaned, although this proved little problem in the Royal Clarence Yard as it was only used for the Royal Train and the Royal waiting rooms were only furnished from naval stores when needed. With the Navy in charge the station was always kept up to scratch and in good order. This may have been the case here, but one does imagine that a lot of cleaning and sweeping went on in and around Gosport and at Fort Brockhurst stations.

Particular attention was paid at Fareham, because it was here that the Royal Train stopped to change engines and reverse. The station master would not want the Royal party looking at an untidy station. All of the stations along the entire route were closed to the public well before the funeral train was due, all signal boxes were double manned, all junctions had hand signalmen stationed at them, all platform edges were lined with railway employees and all unsightly wagons were hidden in secluded sidings. The other station to be affected greatly was Victoria, which closed to the travelling public and normal traffic between 9.00 am and 11.00 am to facilitate the preparations for the arrival of the Royal Train. All the advertisements around the station and all the posters and placards were removed or covered up and parts of the station were cleaned and freshened up.

The official notification and details of the running of the special train to London was contained within a special railway notice of 1st February, 1901. This special notice and other accompanying notices were issued from the office of the superintendent of the line who was based at London Bridge station. Company rivalries were put aside at this time and the notices were issued in the joint names of the London, Brighton & South Coast Railway which ran the line through from Havant to Victoria, and the London & South Western Railway Company (LSWR) which ran the Gosport line and the line through to Farlington Junction. These were the two major railway companies in the South of England and they would be responsible for taking the Queen's remains into London.

The Great Western Railway (GWR) was to be responsible for the section of journey from London to Windsor and this company issued notices separate from those mentioned above. The joint notification (a copy of which can be seen elsewhere in this publication), showed that the train carrying the body of the late Queen also had on board the King and Queen, the German Kaiser, the Royal Princes and other Royal Personages. The train was to run from the Royal Clarence Yard to Fareham, then Cosham, Farlington Junction, Havant, Ford Junction, Horsham, Dorking and Mitcham Junction and then on to London Victoria, and that it would consist of eight vehicles.

All possible details were covered in the railway notices, even the arrangements of the indicator lamps on the front of the locomotives, and there were special procedures noted if the weather should be inclement. The indicator lamp details for the pilot engine, which travelled 15 minutes ahead of the Royal Train to make sure all was well and the line was clear, were the same as those for the Royal Train. This type of train indicator was in common use right up until the end of the use of steam locomotives on British Railways and were there

The funeral train leaving Gosport for London.

to help the signalling and station staff identify different trains from a distance. The instructions used were the standard LB&SCR Royal Train indicators and were fairly simple. The notice stated that if the weather was clear three white boards with a double diamond painted on them were to be shown on the front of the engine: one fixed on top of the smokebox and one each end of the buffer beam. However if the weather was misty or foggy four lights were to be used: a green on top of the smokebox, a green centre of the buffer beam with white ones placed at each end.

Also in this special notice were the working arrangements and the technical railway details for running this very special train. Here suffice it to say that London & South Western engines, crews and guards would be provided from Gosport to Fareham and would be responsible for the running of the train in that section and that the London, Brighton & South Coast Company would take over and provide its own engines, crew and guards from Fareham to Victoria. However, from Fareham to Farlington Junction, both the pilot engine and the train engine were in charge of London & South Western pilotmen as this was still the property of the South Western company. The stretch of line from Farlington to Havant was jointly owned and from Havant onwards the line was the property of the Brighton company.

The advance or pilot engine ran 10 to 15 minutes ahead of the Royal Train to ensure that the track was clear. For the technically minded the details of the Royal Train are as follows. The load was stated as being of about 190 tons when empty and consisted of the five coach LB&SCR Royal Train and the GWR saloon plus the bogie first and bogie first/second composite coaches which were often added to strengthen the Royal Train when extra seating was required. These two extra coaches were fitted between the fifth vehicle of the Royal Train and the saloon brake car. The official notifice was signed by Chas J. Owens, the General Manager of the LSWR, Sam Fay, superintendent of the line for the LSWR, William Forbes, the General Manager LB&SCR and D. Greenwood, the superintendent of the line for the LB&SCR.

The route to be taken was over 110 miles in length of which 10 were by water and 96 by rail, with the rest by road. The London & South Western locomotive allocated to haul the Royal Train from Clarence Yard to Fareham was an Adams 'A12 'class 0-4-2, No. 555, which had been fitted with a Westinghouse pump and was immaculately turned out. William Adams was one of the more likeable of the Victorian engineers. His beginnings were in marine engineering with which he grew up on the London river. He spent time as an engineering officer in the Sardinian Navy during the Garibaldi wars before he took to locomotive engineering, although by the time of the Royal Funeral he had retired from the company some 23 years earlier.

Before the locomotive backed the Royal Train away from the site behind St George barracks where it had spent the night, and slowly dropped back into the Royal Victoria station, the Royal Remains were embarked onto the train, and Sir Michael Culme-Seymour, the late Queen's principal Aide-de-Camp, entered the carriage and with others stood guard over the coffin all the way to London.

When the train reached the Royal Victoria station in Royal Clarence Yard all the dignitaries were ushered to their indicated seats, and this is where

LSWR 'A12 'class 0-4-2, No. 555.   *Gosport Railway Society*

confusion arose and the first delay occurred. It is remarkable that the train was only eight minutes late departing, because most of the official guests were sitting in the wrong places. As already stated the train was to proceed to Fareham where it had to reverse and in so doing the back carriage would become the front carriage and vice versa. Someone had not realised this in Gosport and all the important guests and Royalty were conducted to the incorrect seats. When the mistake had been realised these important personages, who through the strict regime of protocol and rank must sit in the correct places, had to move from one end of the train to the other, so causing the delay.

The irony of the situation was that Queen Victoria always insisted on travelling facing the engine and would never travel facing the other way. Because of the route chosen by the King, for the first five miles of her last journey she had to travel with her back to the engine; we are sure that The Queen would not have been 'amused'.

To drive this first part of the journey, Portsmouth railway depot chose one of its most experienced men and best qualified drivers, George Russell, a man with over 40 years' experience. But as will be stated later it appears that he received no tangible recognition for his services. In fact, on the contrary, he was to be out of pocket. The way Mr Russell's family came to hear of his selection for this very special task was unusual. The first person to find out was Emma, one of his 12 children. Every working day Emma would hurry to Fratton station to meet the 12.25 with her father's dinner and when the engine was shunted into a siding he would sit on the footplate and eat it. At that time it was the proud boast of engine drivers that they did not leave their engines, but stayed to look after them, even during their lunch breaks. The men of the main line railway always felt superior to those who worked the neighbouring branch line to East Southsea; they looked down on these men who actually closed the station while they had their lunch.

One cold morning Emma arrived as usual with her father's dinner and waited for the 12.25, but when the train arrived her father was not driving. Puzzled she asked 'What's happened to Dad?' and a porter explained that he had been sent over to the Royal Clarence Yard to rehearse. 'Rehearse for what?' was the obvious next question, 'For the funeral' was the reply, 'he is to drive the Queen on her last journey'. Sure enough, in Gosport George Russell, and all the other railwaymen who were detailed to be involved in the Royal Funeral, were busy doing dummy runs and making final preparations.

Russell was told that on the day itself he had to wear a new cap and a blue serge suit with a black mourning arm band. The company would provide the new cap but he had to provide the blue serge suit. This was an item that George Russell did not possess and it cost him almost a week's pay to purchase one.

On the day of the funeral George Russell must have felt very proud as he climbed aboard the locomotive, which had been draped in black crepe for the occasion, and he must have been very nervous as he set off on this remarkable (if short) journey. However this was not the only time that George Russell's name hit the headlines because 20 years earlier, in 1881, he was driving the engine *Eclipse* when it became trapped in snow drifts near Ports Creek, after a blizzard. He and his fireman were stuck on the shelterless footplate for over 12 hours as workmen dug in the driving snow to release them. When the train and its passengers were eventually released the snow had reached the height of the carriage roofs and the only way that sustenance could be passed to the passengers was to remove the oil lamps from the roof and pass supplies through the holes. As a result of this snowy event George suffered with foot and hand problems for the rest of his life.

When all had been correctly seated the funeral train eventually left the Royal Clarence Yard. Its route took it past the new sergeant's quarters and allotments at the back of the New Barracks. So as not to offend sensibilities, the occupants were ordered to ensure that no washing was to be hung on any of the washing lines until the funeral train had passed.

There was a further delay at Fareham, when the train reversed and the locomotives were changed. After the normal coupling-up procedure had taken place the brakes were routinely tested and the system failed. This must have been something which caused great embarrassment. The Royal Train fitter (at least one fitter always travelled with the Royal Train) was called and the fault rectified but not before the train was delayed a further 10 minutes. After these delays the driver was told to try to make up time and reach London as soon as possible as the King would be there to meet the train and he was well known for his hatred of unpunctuality.

Empress at Mitcham Common, making her way towards London. The Royal headcode is clearly visible. Note the double-acting signal in the background.   *Klaus Marx*

The LB&SCR Royal Train on a happier occasion, at Epsom Downs station on Derby Day 1908. The locomotive is the brand-new 'I2' class 4-4-2T No. 15. The 12-wheel Royal Saloon is in the centre of the five-car formation. The train awaits the return of King Edward VII.   *Charles Long*

A very poor quality picture of the funeral train approaching South London.

Gosport Railway Society

The Official Schedule of the Royal Train was as follows:

	Arrive am	Pass am	Depart am
Gosport Royal Clarence Yard			8.45
Gosport		8.48	
Fareham (reverse)	8.54		8.58
Cosham		9.07	
Farlington Junction		9.10	
Havant Junction		9.15	
Bosham		9.21	
Chichester		9.25	
Barnham Junction		9.32	
Ford Junction		9.36	
Arundel		9.40	
Amberley		9.44	
Hardham Junction		9.49	
Pulborough		9.50	
Billingshurst		9.56	
Horsham		10.05	
Warnham		10.08	
Dorking		10.23	
Leatherhead Junction		10.28	
Epsom Junction		10.33	
Sutton Junction		10.38	
Mitcham Junction		10.43	
Balham Junction Main Line		10.50	
Clapham Junction		10.54	
Grosvenor Road (reduced speed)		10.58	
Victoria	11.00		

As well as making up the time which had been lost in the Gosport and Fareham area, the LB&SC driver from Fareham (Walter Cooper), actually managed to gain time and the train arrived at Victoria two minutes early. This must have resulted in some very spirited and lively running. Time was regained throughout the duration of the journey and it is understood that an estimated speed of 80 mph was attained on the flat, level section between Havant and Ford Junction. This is another fact that would not have 'amused' Her Majesty as she always insisted on travelling at a moderate speed and was supplied with a

LB&SCR No. 54 *Empress* in the funeral drapes which it carried for the Fareham to Victoria section of the funeral journey. *The Locomotive Magazine*

way map or chart on all her railway journeys. This way map showed the main points of interest along the route which she was travelling, the place names and passing times; if she felt that the train was travelling too fast she would make sure that the railway staff were informed and were told to slow the train down to a 'respectable speed'.

Certain railway officers who were officially travelling on board the Royal Train thought that a maximum speed of 92 mph was attained whilst it was running down Holmwood Bank. The reverse curve at Dorking, which was at the bottom of the hill and had a restriction of 30 mph, must have caused moments of real anxiety. In hindsight, and with a careful study of the facts and timings which are available, one does tend to accept that the speed running down the bank did not exceed more than 70 mph, although the rough riding of the two Royal Brake Saloons might well have given the impression of a much higher speed.

For the railway companies, William Willcox, the northern district engineer was in the first brake and Mr Constable, the brake inspector, was in the other. Mr Willcox claimed that the higher speed was attained but Mr Constable argued that the speed never exceeded 75 mph. So much for the evidence of expert witnesses!

When asked for his opinion, J. Pelham Maitland of the locomotive running department, who was also on the train, stated that from his own experience as a fireman on this particular line a certain amount of rough riding always developed about ¾ mile south of Dorking tunnel. He attributed this to the spongy foundations on which the track was laid. This, plus the rough riding of the vehicles, could have given the somewhat false impression of 90 mph when in reality it was only 75. At this point a sharp application of the train brakes was needed before the locomotive entered the tunnel (as was the normal practice when a train was running late and trying to make up time), then the negotiation of the curve at between 40 and 45 miles per hour, which was probably the speed at which the funeral train was moving by then, could lead to an impression of speed faster than it actually was.

Ahead of the funeral train was the pilot engine the LB&SCR No. 53 named *Sirdar*, the second of the Billinton 'B4' class to be built. Mr Billinton himself was on the footplate of No. 54 *Empress* which pulled the Royal Funeral Train and was accompanied by the outdoor locomotive superintendent, Mr J. Richardson. Both men commented that it was a splendid trip although bitterly cold. The cold weather was, later in the day, to have a lasting effect on the conduct of all State Funerals in the future. Besides the General Managers and the Chief Officers, Lord Cottessloe and Colonel Campbell, Chairmen of the LB&SCR and the LSWR respectively, were on the train representing the interests of their companies.

One of the most outstanding things that was noted by many of the passengers was that as the train passed many people were seen kneeling at the lineside. Much interest was shown in the running of the train and the Kaiser was greatly interested in the performance of the locomotive and, after the arrival at Victoria, sent one of his equerries to express his views to the driver (Walter Cooper) and the fireman (F. Way). The Kaiser was most impressed and stated that this journey was a remarkable achievement for such a small locomotive as compared with those used in Germany.

Funeral train at Carshalton. *Railway Magazine*

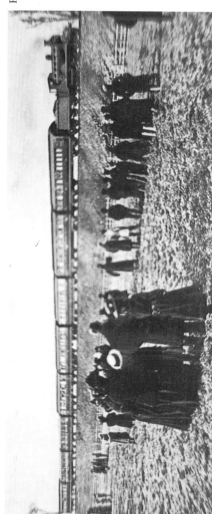

Funeral train *en route* from
Gosport to Victoria.
Railway Magazine

Chapter Three

The People of the Capital Pay their Respects

The Royal coffin was removed from the carriage by an officer and 12 men of the Guards and Household Calvary and placed upon a gun carriage. From Victoria the coffin was conveyed through the streets of London to Paddington station so that the people could pay their last respects to their Queen. The procession was led by an officer of the Household and details of the procession can be seen in the Appendix.

In London everywhere were the signs of grief and most people exhibited some signs of the national sense of personal loss. As the day wore on hardly a shop was open that did not display a mourning board, while the driver of every public vehicle had a knot of crêpe attached to his whip. The official signs of mourning were displayed with the usual solemnity; flags flew at half-mast from public buildings and from many private establishments, and to a large extent business in the City was suspended.

At a 11.15 the cortège passed by Buckingham Palace where a Guard of Honour was mounted. The coffin was pulled by eight cream horses and was draped in a white pall, as was the Queen's wish, and on top was laid the Imperial Crown, Orb, Sceptre and the Collar of the Order of the Garter. The procession weaved its way through the streets of London on its way to Paddington. The silence of the crowd was almost tangible, there were no demonstrations and few sounds were heard save for the firing of the mourning guns, the jingle of the horses' harnesses, the rattle of ceremonial swords and the clatter of the horses' hooves as they slowly walked along.

Servicemen in the procession consisted of 300 sailors from Portsmouth and Chatham, and 300 Royal Marine Light Infantrymen plus 100 Royal Marine Artillerymen and the Royal Marine Band from Chatham. Their comfort and needs had not been ignored. Arrangements had been made for the whole of this contingent, both the officers and the men, to be catered for at the famous Trocadero Restaurant. Here the procession party were supplied with refreshments and it is reported that the accommodation left nothing to be desired and that the conduct of the men could not have been more orderly.

As the cortège passed through the streets the crowds that lined the way were immense, but they all waited in reverence, patience and silence and in some areas were over 100 people deep. All was quiet as the procession passed by and there was no cheering.

The buildings along the route were draped in purple, unfortunately not all in the same shade which gave a somewhat mottled appearance in places. Stands were erected at the roadside from Marlborough House right up to Marble Arch and even the lamposts were garlanded with ribbons.

All house blinds were raised, which was totally against Victorian tradition, but the request to leave them open came directly from the King. The weather was still not bright, but when the procession passed through the gates at Hyde Park Corner a rift in the clouds allowed a shaft of sunlight to play down on the

The gentlemen prepare to move the coffin from the train at Victoria station.

Navy & Army Illustrated

The white draped coffin passes through the streets of London.   *London Illustrated News*

Sat astride his charger the King follows the coffin of his Late Mother as the procession
progresses through the streets.   *London Illustrated News*

Above: A nation's capital pays its respects as the funeral gun carriage passes through the streets of London.

Top right: The King, the Kaiser and the Duke of Connaught entering Paddington station.

The Sphere

Right: Marching into Paddington station.

The Sphere

Queen Alexandra leaves her carriage at Paddington station ready for the Windsor leg of the funeral journey.

uniforms and shining ceremonial armour below. The weather being as it was cloaks and greatcoats were the order of the day, somewhat taking away the splendour of the procession.

On arrival at Paddington the last stage of the journey was to begin. Stands had been erected on the approaches to the entrance of the arrival platforms and were draped in purple and white. The wall along this side of the station was covered in red cloth over which hung large loops of purple and white.

A stand was erected on platform No. 9 and the bridge which crossed the station was decorated with drapes and crowded with mourners and spectators. For there was nothing the Victorians liked better than the spectacle of a State occasion whether it be a wedding, official visit or funeral. The funeral train was drawn up at arrival platform No. 8 along which was placed a thick red carpet flanked by white flowers and with potted palms along the walls.

The Great Western Funeral Train

The Great Western Funeral Train was composed of the Queen's saloon No. 2 which was sited in the middle of the train and contained the coffin, four saloons, one first class corridor coach and two vans. Carriage No. 229 had been taken to Portsmouth on the previous Wednesday night so it could be included in the LB&SC rake of Royal Train stock. Then having completed the journey to Victoria and after the coffin had been removed, it was taken from the Royal rake and hauled around to Paddington to be included in the Great Western Royal Train.

Because of the slowness of the procession across London, the head of the procession did not arrive at Paddington station until 12.30 pm. A correspondent to the *Railway Gazette* many years later, stated that by a series of unusual events (unfortunately he does not elaborate on this) he found himself on the platform right next to the funeral saloon in line with six Royal personages and not far from King Edward and the German Emperor. From this position he watched the coffin being removed from the gun-carriage by eight sergeants from the Guards Regiments and placed aboard the train, while the massed bands play Chopin's 'Funeral March'. As soon as the Great Western guard had locked the doors of the funeral saloon this correspondent heard King Edward say to the German Emperor 'Come on, hurry up, we are almost 20 minutes late already', whereupon the whole Royal Party then entrained with great speed. During the arrival and entrainment of the coffin and the Royal mourners the military bands played the 'Funeral March' and continued to do so until the train had left and was out of sight.

An account in *Lloyds Weekly Newspaper* of 3rd February, 1901 states that the funeral train left at 1.40 pm, whereas the account in the *Railway Magazine* of March 1901 gives the departure time as 1.32 pm (and this is borne out by GWR records). The funeral train was immediately preceded by another train conveying Earl Roberts and the GHQ staff of the Army. This was hauled by 'Atbara' class 4-4-0 No. 3374 *Baden Powell* and acted as 'Pilot' to the funeral train. Other special trains with guests, Cabinet Ministers, Ambassadors and other members of the Diplomatic Corps had left earlier.

GREAT WESTERN RAILWAY.

FUNERAL

OF

𝕳er late 𝕸ajesty 𝕼ueen 𝖁ictoria

On SATURDAY, FEBRUARY 2nd, 1901,

The Train Service throughout the Great Western Company's system will be the same as on Sundays, with the following modifications, viz. :—

The 5.30 a.m. and 5.40 a.m. Newspaper Trains from Paddington will run as usual as far as Plymouth and Swansea respectively, with connections to the Weymouth Line, Torquay, Kingswear and Penzance, and also to Oxford, Birmingham, Wolverhampton, Dudley, Worcester, Malvern, &c.

The 12.0 night Train from Paddington to Penzance, and the 12.15 night Train from Paddington to Birmingham, Chester, Birkenhead and Liverpool will run as usual.

LONDON AND WINDSOR SERVICE.

The 1.0 p.m. Sunday Train from Paddington to Windsor will not run.

The 10.30 a.m., 10.35 a.m., 1.50 p.m. and 2.20 p.m. Sunday Trains from Paddington will not convey passengers to Windsor.

Windsor Station will be closed for public traffic from 11.0 a.m. until 2.30 p.m.

LONDON SUBURBAN SERVICE.

The following Trains will run as on Week Days in addition to the usual Sunday service :—

8.0 a.m. Southall to Paddington.

7.45 a.m. Windsor to Paddington.

8.0 a.m. Reading to Paddington.

8.50 a.m. Southall to Paddington.

8.53 a.m. Uxbridge to Paddington.

A Train will run from Southall to Paddington at 10.0 a.m., calling at intermediate Stations.

The 11.25 a.m. Sunday Train from High Wycombe to Paddington will be half an hour later at all Stations.

SAILINGS—NEW MILFORD AND WATERFORD.

There will be no Steamer from Waterford to New Milford on Friday, February 1st, nor from New Milford to Waterford on Sunday morning, February 3rd.

The issue of Week-end Excursion Tickets to Windsor and the Half-day Excursion Tickets to London will be suspended.

For particulars of any additional Local arrangements on other parts of the Line, see Special announcements issued locally.

J. L. WILKINSON, General Manager.

Paddington Station, January, 1901.

Notice to the public re altered train services.   *Oakwood Press Collection*

The funeral train itself was crammed with European Royalty, particularly from Germany. The chief foreign mourner was the German Kaiser and, to emphasise his own importance, he had seen to it that nine officers and men from Queen Victoria's Own German Regiment (she was Honorary Colonel in Chief of the 1st Dragoon Guards), and four men from the 5th Blucher Hussars (of which King Edward was Colonel) came to the funeral. So at very short notice the Great Western company had to find seating accommodation to transport them to Windsor. They travelled in the semi-saloon of the trailing brake van.

For this solemn occasion the locomotive chosen to haul the Royal Train was an 'Atbara' class 4-4-0 locomotive, named *Royal Sovereign* specially for the occasion. The locomotive was actually the newly-overhauled locomotive No. 3373 *Atbara* but it temporarily carried the name, but not the number plates, of its sister engine No. 3050. This was done as it was thought that the name was more suitable for this occasion.

The locomotive was heavily draped along the sides of the boiler with wide purple ribbons and the Royal Coat of Arms was also draped in ribbons. The locomotive carried a wreath of white flowers with purple streamers with the Royal monogram VR in the centre attached to the smokebox door. To this day the wreath is in the Great Western Museum in Swindon (now 'Steam'). To represent the Great Western Railway Company, Earl Cawdor, who was the Chairman, and Mr J.L. Wilkinson, who was the General Manager, travelled on the Royal Train from Paddington to Windsor.

A contemporary report in *The Times* on the Queen's saloon stated that:

> The sumptuous divans and revolving fauteuils had been removed and in their place an imposing catafalque about two foot high and equipped with four huge white leather straps. The whole was draped in purple and ornamented with white satin rosettes. The interior of the compartment, from which the partitions had been removed, was entirely upholstered in white satin. Broad purple strips divided the walls into panels crowned with a purple garland and held in place by white rosettes and ribbons.

As with the journey south of London the whole length of this section of the route was lined and guarded by picked men who had been drawn from all ranks of working men within the Great Western Railway Company. These linesmen were positioned on both sides of the track and were placed at about 25 yard intervals to be within sight and hearing of each other so that messages could be passed if required.

The same rules with regard to spectators also applied here, but, as in the South, this did not prevent large crowds turning out to pay their last respects and to kneel, with heads bowed, at the trackside as the Royal Train passed.

A Great Western admission ticket to Paddington station to view the Royal Funeral train's departure.

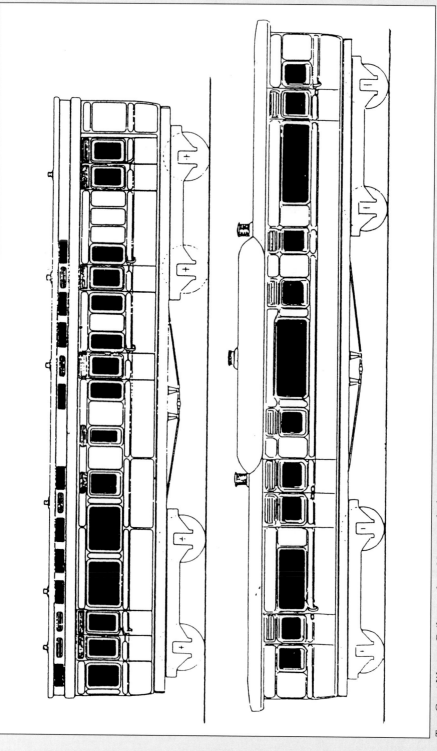

Top: Great Western Railway saloon No. 229 which carried Queen Victoria's coffin from Gosport to London Victoria.
Above: Great Western Railway Royal saloon No. 2 which carried Queen Victoria's coffin from Paddington to Windsor.

Everyone on the train had to be in their own special places allocated according to their station in life. Set out below are the travel arrangements and seating plan for the mourners aboard the Royal Funeral Train as it left Paddington at 1.32 pm on Saturday 2nd February, 1901, over ½ hour later than scheduled.
The train consisted of a locomotive and eight carriages thus:

Locomotive	J. Armstrong; inspector W. Greenaway,
Royal Sovereign	driver D. Hughes, fireman G. Bayliss

(1) First Brake Semi-Saloon

Royal brake van	Guard T. King, W.H. Waister, E. Rendell
Royal semi-saloon	Royal footmen and attendants

(2) First Corridor and (3) Saloon

Compartments	A. Hubbard, Mr Robinson, T.I. Allen, W.A. Hart (GWR)	
Saloon	Lt Col Sir A. Bigge	Col H.H. Mathias
(of the two vehicles)	Col W. Aitken	Col E.T. Hutton
	Lt Col Rt Hon. Sir F.I. Edwards	Col J. Brocklehurst
	Lt Col Hon. W.P. Carington	Capt. Sir E. Chichester
	Lt Col A. Davidson	Capt. E.S. Poe
	Lt Col Hon. H.C. Legge	Capt. Count F.C. Metaxa
	Capt. F. Ponsonby	Capt. W.H. May
	Sir J. Reid	Col B.G.D. Cooke
	Lord Suffield	Col Lord Blythswood
	Lord Lawrence	Col J.H. Rivett-Carnac
	Lord Churchill	Col J. Stevenson
	Lord Colville of Culross	Col Earl of Harewood
	Col Brabazon	Col Duke of Beaufort
	Col H. Ricardo	Col C.B. Bashford
	Col J.C. Cavendish	Col Earl of March
	Col Sir R. Ogilvy	Col Duke of Montrose
	Col Duke of Northumberland	Brevet-Col T.F.D. Bridge
	Col Marquis of Londonderry	Col H.N. McRae
	Col Earl of Haddington	Col H.G. Dixon
	Col Viscount Galway	Col G.L.C. Money
	Col C.P. Le Cornu	Col H. Lampton
	Col J. Davis	Capt. C. Campbell
	Col W. Martin	Capt. A. Macleod
	Col W. Bell	Capt. A.A.C. Parr
	Col W. Campbell	Capt. G.L. Atkinson

(4) The Royal Saloon

THE COFFIN OF HER LATE MOST GRACIOUS MAJESTY

Flanked by

The Duke of Portland	The Duke of Norfolk
The Earl of Clarendon	The Earl of Pembroke

A very poor quality photograph of Queen Victoria's GWR funeral train journeying to Windsor.
Railway Magazine

Royal Sovereign, ready for the Queen's last railway journey.   *Locomotive Magazine*

Right: The schedule for the guests' trains, which was not adhered to because of the lateness of the procession in arriving at Paddington.   *Public Record Office*

GREAT WESTERN RAILWAY.

No. 14. (For the use of the Company's Servants only.)

Notice of Special Passenger Trains

BETWEEN

PADDINGTON & WINDSOR

ON

SATURDAY, FEBRUARY 2nd, 1901,

FOR THE

Conveyance of Guests proceeding to the Funeral Service of Her Majesty Queen Victoria.

TIME TABLE OF DOWN TRAINS.

	No. 1 Special	No. 2 Special	No. 3 Special	No. 4 Special	R.R. Special
	From No. 1 Platform.	From No. 3 Platform.	From No. 1 Platform.	From No. 9 Platform.	From No. 6 Platform.
	NOON	P.M.	P.M.	P.M. about	An additional Special will stand in readiness at No. 6 Platform to follow the Royal Train if required.
PADDINGTON ... ... dep.	12 0	12 10	12 30	12 50	
SOUTHALL ... ... pass	12 13	12 23	12 43	See Note	
SLOUGH ... ... pass	12 24	12 34	12 54	*	
WINDSOR ... ... arr.	12 30	12 40	1 0	Below	

⁎ No. 4 Special Train will leave Paddington about 10 minutes in advance of the Royal Train (see Notice No. 12) and **must be regarded as the "Pilot" to the Royal Train, and the instructions contained in Royal Train Notice No. 12, so far as they concern the "Pilot" Service for the Royal Train, must be strictly observed in working this Train.** It will start from No. 9 Platform and run along the Down Engine and Carriage Line, passing on to the Down Main Line at Subway Junction in the same manner as shewn in Notice No. 12 for the Royal Train—the speed between Paddington and Subway Junction must not exceed ten miles per hour, and the Train will occupy the same time in running between Paddington and Windsor as the Royal Train.

RETURN SPECIAL TRAINS.

The Special Trains will return from Windsor after the Funeral as may be required, probably between 3.15 p.m. and 4.30 p.m. The Staff at all Stations must be on the look-out for Telegraphic Advice of the starting of the Special Trains from Windsor, and the Line must be kept clear for them.

GENERAL INSTRUCTIONS.

For General Instructions to be observed in connection with the running of Special Trains, see pages 95 to 100 of Appendix to Book of Rules and Regulations, and for Special Instructions to be observed in connection with the working of the "Pilot" Service to the Royal Train see Royal Train Notice No. 12.

Receipt of this Notice to be acknowledged to Head of Department by **WIRE.**

T. I. ALLEN,

PADDINGTON, FEBRUARY 1st, 1901. *Superintendent of the Line.*

'Atbara' class 4-4-0 No. 3374 *Baden Powell* hauling the special train ('No. 4 Special' in Notice 14 - see *illustration page* 63) which acted as pilot to the funeral train from Paddington to Windsor on 2nd February. Notice the special Royal headlamp beneath the chimney.

Dr T.F. Budden/Roger Carpenter Collection

(4) The Royal Saloon (continued)

Maj. Gen. Sir H. Ewart	Major Count Gleichen
Maj. Gen. Sir J. McNeill	Lord Belper
Capt. HSH Prince Louis of Battenberg	F.M. The Rt. Hon. Viscount Wolseley
Adml Sir M. Culme-Seymour	Viscount Valentia
Sir A. Acland Hood Bart.	Duke of Buccleuch
Earl of Waldegrave	V. Cavendish Esq.
Lt Col H.T. Fenwick	Vice Adml Sir J. Fullerton

(5) Saloon

HM The King	HM The Queen
HRH The Duke of Connaught	HRH The Duchess of Fife
HIM The Kaiser	HRH Princess Victoria
HRH The Duke of Saxe-Coburg	HRH Princess Charles of Denmark
Crown Prince of Germany	HRH Princess Christian
Prince Arthur of Connaught	HRH Duchess of Argyll
Prince Henry of Prussia	HRH Princess Henry of Battenberg
The Crown Prince of Denmark	HIH Duchess of Saxe-Coburg
Prince Charles of Denmark	HRH Duchess of Connaught
	HRH Duchess of Albany
	HRH Princess Adolf of Schaumberg-Lippe

(6) Saloon   Chiefly foreign Royalty

(7) Saloon   Ladies whose husbands were elsewhere in the train and the late Queen's close female personal staff.

(8) First Brake Semi-Saloon   German Army deputation
Earl Cawdor & Mr J.L. Wilkinson (GWR)
Guard W.J. Fowler and Interpreters

To the series of mishaps that had marred the day must be added one more, details of which appear below. The station arrangements at Windsor were under the direction of the assistant superintendent Mr Morris. The waiting rooms were filled with the choicest blooms, the platform carpeted and the iron columns hidden by marguerites and tapering palms. All the plants were furnished from the Royal Gardens. When the train drew in and came to a stand the troops and seamen presented arms. The Royal party alighted and the white leather straps holding the coffin to the catafalque were slowly released. Then to the sound of sombre music the coffin was carried from the train by non-commissioned officers from the First Grenadier Guards headed by Lt Seymour. The coffin was carried across the platform and placed on the khaki gun carriage waiting on the carriage road. The coffin was then covered in a white embroidered pall upon which the Royal crown, sceptre and orbs were laid.

The work of the railway companies was now complete and later that year there were to be awards for at least one of the employees. The driver of the Great Western train, David Hughes, who had regularly driven the Queen over Great Western metals for many years was, in July of that year, awarded the medal of the Royal Victorian Order by King Edward VII. However, we can find no record as to whether any like awards were ever made to the LSWR driver Russell or the LB&SC driver Cooper and the other train staff.

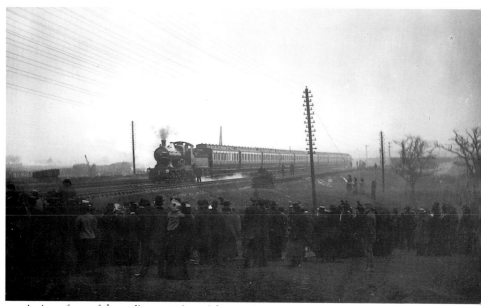

A view of one of the earlier guests' specials near Acton.
Dr T.F. Budden/Roger Carpenter Collection

Queen Victoria's funeral train, hauled by 'Atbara' class No. 3373, renamed *Royal Sovereign* for the event, and with a wreath on the smokebox and Royal coat of arms on the side near Acton, 2nd February, 1901.   *Dr T.F. Budden/Graham Carpenter Collection*

It was now that the final mishap of the day occurred. It was a typical crisp February morning and the hawsers and traces which had been provided to haul the gun carriage from the station to the castle were stiff, brittle and in some cases frozen. The horses which were to pull the gun carriage had been waiting a long time and had become restive whilst standing around in the intense cold and it was deemed that they were too highly strung to perform the task. A solution had to be found and quickly. After a fruitless search for replacement hawsers and traces a compromise had to be found, so the communication cords were stripped out of a rake of Great Western carriages berthed nearby. Also, after another search, no other suitable horses were to be found and so an alternative form of power was required. The route was lined with servicemen and they were the obvious choice. The first detachment were the men of the Royal Navy and Admiral Sir Michael Culme-Seymour, standing close by, shouted reassuringly as the sailors fell in fore and aft of the gun carriage: 'My boys will put things right'.

Presumably the Admiral had first obtained permission from the King to use the sailors. The communication cords were then connected to the back of the gun carriage to act as a drag brake. Before the sailors could manhandle the gun carriage away the artillery officers and their horses were instructed to clear the road. One can well imagine that this was far from popular with their Commanding Officer, Lt Col. Sir A. Bigge, who accused the Admiral of 'deliberately ruining the ceremony'.

This simple act has set a precedent and to this day the Navy jealously guard the right to haul the gun carriage at a State Funeral. Unfortunately by the time all this reorganisation had taken place, the head of the procession, unaware of the problems at the rear, had set off at the appointed time and an NCO had to run ahead to stop the procession until all was ready.

From nine o'clock that morning special trains had brought in hundreds of mourners from London and other neighbouring towns. Earlier in the day a train load of police constables and sergeants had arrived to assist the local police force with crowd management, in what was graphically described in the local paper the following week as 'a seething mass of humanity all dressed in sombre colours and mourning'. People were clinging to every possible vantage point, lamp posts, trees, roofs, walls and fences. The town's ambulances were kept busy rescuing and treating members of the public who had fainted or been crushed.

There were so many people present that, at the request of the local council, the King ordered the route of the procession to be lengthened so that as many of the ordinary people as possible could pay their respects. The procession formed up and the 5th Blucher Hussars marched off and at 1 o'clock the mayor and civic dignitaries plus Sir Francis Trees Barry, Bart MP, the Recorder and the Clerk of the Peace left from outside the Guildhall.

Eventually the procession pulled away from the station and slowly threaded its way through the streets of Windsor. Along the route behind the military guard were people standing many deep to view the procession.

The gun carriage was followed by the official mourners most of whom were on foot and these were led by the King and the Kaiser. Many of the older and

Right: The gun carriage, which had been specially fitted with pneumatic tyres for the occasion. *The Sphere*

Below: The funeral procession prepares to leave the Great Western station at Windsor. *Navy & Army Illustrated*

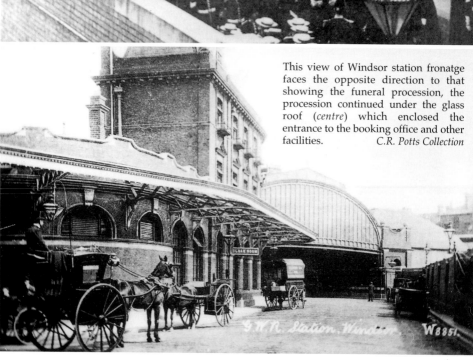

This view of Windsor station fronatge faces the opposite direction to that showing the funeral procession, the procession continued under the glass roof (*centre*) which enclosed the entrance to the booking office and other facilities. *C.R. Potts Collection*

The arrival of the funeral train at Windsor: Queen Alexandra entering her carriage at the railway station.

The Queen's last homecoming: the funeral procession entering the castle grounds at Windsor.

The Royal Navy take the strain and the last Queen Empress in her own right is taken through the streets of Windsor.   *Author's Collection*

less able mourners struggled but were determined to walk the whole distance, such people as the ailing Duke of Cambridge who manfully struggled along leaning very heavily on the arm of his son Adolphus for most of the time. The one member of the Royal Family who was missing was the Duke of York who was still recovering from measles.

The cortège passed through the town and made its way on through the Long Walk gate which is situated on the end of the three mile, tree-lined avenue, leading to Windsor Castle. This part of the route was lined by boys and Masters from Eton College, the late Queen's servants and their families, Crown Officials and the employees of Windsor Great Park. There were also children from the Royal Schools and other local school children.

On reaching the castle the procession entered through the Sovereign's Entrance, crossed the quadrangle and so on to St George's Chapel. At the entrance to the Chapel the Royal Remains were received by the Dean and Prebendaries and the Choir of Windsor, who fell in immediately behind the Heralds. The procession, which included the Knights of the several Orders wearing their respective Collars with White Rosettes, moved into the Chapel where a large congregation had been waiting (inside) for a long time. They were shivering with the cold as the Chapel heating was not working properly. Those inside witnessed the coffin being ceremonially brought through the great West doors and laid to rest in the choir. All members of the procession were instructed that they were to wear full dress with a band of crêpe four inches broad on the left arm, cloaks or greatcoats could he worn but not mackintoshes.

Here in the Chapel the Queen lay amidst the effigies of the Prince Consort, Prince Leopold and Prince Eddy. She was also surrounded by the gold fringed standards of the Knights of the Order of the Garter as they hung over the richly carved stalls. The King, being the Chief Mourner stood at the head of the coffin and the Lord Chamberlain of His Majesty's Household stood at the foot with the Lord Steward on his right and the Earl Marshal on his left. A short service was held using the standard form of service from the *Book of Common Prayer* up to the Interment. The anthem *Blest are the Departed* by Spohr was then sung. The service was conducted by the Archbishop of Canterbury and the Bishop of Winchester. Then William Henry Weldon Esq., Deputy to Garter Principal King of Arms, pronounced the Styles of the Late Queen.

After the solemn benediction by the Archbishop the coffin was carried through into the Albert Memorial Chapel to lie in state ready to be conveyed to the mausoleum at Frogmore on the following Monday. A Guard of Honour was set, a guard which was to stay watching over the coffin continously both day and night until its final journey to Frogmore in two days' time. The fragrance and brilliance of the floral tributes which arrived from all over the world were said to beggar description.

The correct title of the Chapel is 'The Queen's Chapel of St George within her Castle of Windsor', it is a Royal Peculiar and was founded in 1348 by Edward III and is exempt from diocesan jurisdictions. It is a self-governing secular community of priests and laymen. The present chapel was built in 1475 by Edward IV in honour of the Virgin Mary, St George and St Edward. It is here that the Order of the Garter have their stall and insignia within the choir. Over

The Royal gun carriage arrives at the foot of the steps of St George's Chapel Windsor. Note the sailors with their uniform straw hats.
London Illustrated News

The coffin makes its dignified way to St George's Chapel.
London Illustrated News

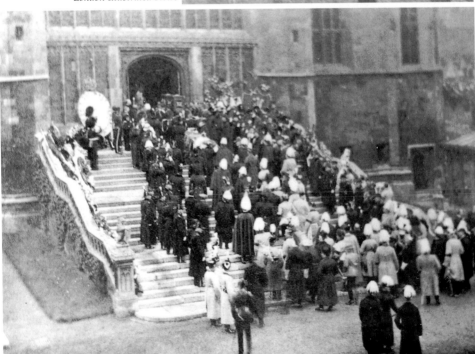

Above: Guardsmen stand watch over the Lying in State in the Albert Memorial Chapel in St George's Windsor.
London Illustrated News

Left: The front cover of the *Navy and Army Illustrated* on Saturday 9th February, 1901.

BURIAL OF THE DEAD

St. GEORGE'S CHAPEL.

WINDSOR CASTLE,

Saturday, 2nd February, 1901

FUNERAL OF HER LATE MAJESTY QUEEN VICTORIA.

2nd February, 1901.

———◆———

Programme of Music.

THE SENTENCES	*Croft.*
PSALM XC.	*Felton.*

THE LESSON.

"MAN THAT IS BORN"	*S. S. Wesley.*
"THOU KNOWEST LORD"	*Purcell.*

(These two though part of the Service are really Anthems.)

THE LORD'S PRAYER	*Gounod*
"HOW BLEST ARE THEY"	*Tschaikowsky.*

(Between the two Collects after Lord's Prayer.)

"How blest are they whom Thou hast chosen, and
taken unto Thee, O Lord.
Their memorial is from generation to generation :
Alleluia ! Alleluia ! Alleluia ! "

After Garter's Proclamation.

ANTHEM . . " Blest are the departed " . .	*Spohr.*

" Blest are the departed, who in the Lord are
sleeping : from henceforth for evermore : they rest
from their labours, and their works follow them."

FUNERAL MARCH	*Beethoven.*

WINDSOR CASTLE.

VISITORS' LIST.

Saturday, February 2nd, 1901.

THEIR MAJESTIES THE KING AND QUEEN	Edward III. Tower
MISS KNOLLYS :...	352, Chintz Room
GENERAL SIR DIGHTON PROBYN	335, York Tower
SIR FRANCIS KNOLLYS	331, Sir William Jenner's Room
CAPTAIN HOLFORD	429, North Front
HIS IMPERIAL MAJESTY THE GERMAN EMPEROR...	State Rooms
HIS EXCELLENCY GENERAL VON PLESSEN	The Lord Chamberlain's Room
HIS EXCELLENCY COUNT METTERNICH	The Lord Steward's Room
LIEUT.-COLONEL THE HON. W. CARINGTON	The Lord in Waiting's Room
HIS MAJESTY THE KING OF THE HELLENES	The Tapestry Rooms
THE GENTLEMAN IN ATTENDANCE........................	433, North Front
HIS ROYAL HIGHNESS THE CROWN PRINCE OF⎱ GERMANY..⎰	State Room
COLONEL VON PRITZELWITZ	449, West Front
LIEUT.-COLONEL THE HON. H. C. LEGGE	Winchester Tower
HIS IMPERIAL HIGHNESS THE GRAND DUKE⎱ MICHAEL OF RUSSIA...⎰	343, Sitting Room, Minister's Rooms
GENTLEMEN IN ATTENDANCE........................	431, North Front
HIS ROYAL HIGHNESS THE CROWN PRINCE OF⎱ DENMARK ....⎰	Tapestry Rooms
THE GENTLEMEN IN ATTENDANCE........................	432, North Front
H.R.H. THE DUKE OF SPARTA.................................	344, Minister's Rooms
H.R.H. PRINCE HENRY OF PRUSSIA........................	State Rooms
ADMIRAL BARON VON SECKENDORFF	446, West Front
ADMIRAL OF THE FLEET SIR EDMUND COMMERELL	Winchester Tower
THEIR ROYAL HIGHNESSES THE DUKE AND⎱ DUCHESS OF CONNAUGHT....................................⎰	235, York Tower
H R.H. PRINCE ARTHUR OF CONNAUGHT.............	172, Edward III. Tower
T.R.H. THE PRINCESSES MARGARET AND VICTORIA⎱ PATRICIA OF CONNAUGHT ....⎰	176, Edward III. Tower
COLONEL AND THE HON. MRS. EGERTON..............	646 and 647, Round Tower
MISS MILNE	649, Round Tower

The Official Visitors' List for the castle.

the years, the Chapel has seen a great many royal funerals and within its vaults lie six of England's rulers and elsewhere in the Chapel lie four others.

The guard was alternately manned by men from the Grenadier Guards and the Royal Bodyguard of Gentlemen-at-Arms, the Life Guards. These guards who stood one at each corner of the coffin, with their rifles reversed and heads bowed, were changed every hour. Before the handover, the senior man of the outgoing Old Guard would charge the senior officer of the incoming New Guard with the words: 'I commit to you the charge of the body of her late Majesty Queen Victoria, Queen of Great Britain and Ireland, Empress of India, together with the Regalia of the British Empire'.

With all the events of the day and the interment of the Queen next to her husband in the mausoleum at Frogmore due two days later, Windsor Castle was to be the host location for many Royal personages and dignitaries from many parts of Europe and from all over the world. It was not just the dignitaries but also their retinues and attendants which they brought along with them. Rooms and accommodation had to be found for them all within the castle. The close family and their special guests were accommodated, as usual, within the Royal Apartments and the official suites, but elsewhere within the castle there seemed to be guests in every room and corner. The castle must have been almost bursting at the seams.

To give an indication of the large number of people who were staying in the castle at this time the dining lists for the day make particularly interesting reading, and probably the caterer's nightmare. It is recorded that 70 royal relations sat down to lunch that day in the main castle dining room and between 600 and 700 other guests (one would have expected more accuracy than this) were seated in St George's Hall. But this was not all, the King's own Royal Household which numbered 24 had also to be fed and accommodated.

Opposite is reproduced a copy of the official Visitors' List for Windsor Castle that day in February 1901, but it is as well to bear in mind that this only details the very important official guests and not of those of lower rank and class, who would be on a separate list.

Windsor Castle from the river, a postcard posted in 1909.   *C.R. Potts Collection*

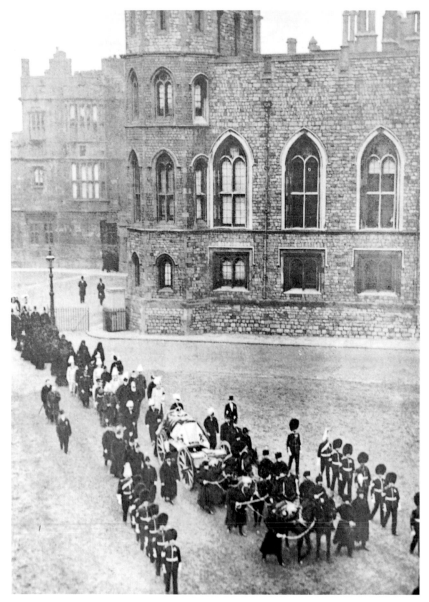

The funeral procession leaves the castle walls at Windsor at three o'clock on 4th February, 1901.   *The Sphere*

Chapter Four

The Final Journey

The following morning, Sunday 3rd February, at 11 o'clock all the Royal Family in residence and the majority of their guests and their retinues had walked across the Quadrangle to attend divine service which was held in St George's Chapel. The principal clerical figure at the service was the Bishop of Oxford who also preached that morning. After the service was over the Royal party, their guests and retinue returned to the castle where luncheon had been prepared for them.

For the majority of the time whilst the Queen was in the Chapel the remains were guarded and the Chapel was closed to the public, but somehow the security at the Chapel must have been breached, possibly with the very best of intentions, when the verger let two lads from nearby Eton College into the Chapel so that they could take a quick look at the coffin. Later in that week an interesting poem appeared in the Eton College magazine, a poem written by one of the lads in which were detailed the feelings they both had after viewing the coffin.

The next morning, Monday 4th February, dawned dull and with a very cold wind. This was the day of the interment, the final part of Queen Victoria's journey to join her beloved Albert. Within the castle walls most of the morning was occupied with making the final arrangements for the short journey, through the Great Park, to the Prince Albert Mausoleum at Frogmore. The coffin was lifted from its resting place in St George's Chapel, and then preceded by the Bishop of Winchester, was carried down the steps outside the great West door by non-commissioned officers of the Guards and was once again set down onto a gun carriage covered with a beautiful white pall. As the clock struck 3 o'clock the procession set off. The gun carriage was pulled by six black horses. The old personal servants of the late Queen were given a position just in front of the coffin, and the Military Knights of Windsor, in full dress, watched the departure of the cortège while the bell in the Great Tower toiled. The bell was made in Moscow and brought from Sebastopol in 1855 and is only used on the death of a sovereign.

The Bishop of Winchester preceded the coffin and the royal personages followed behind in a procession which was not of great length and was devoid of the glitter of uniforms. Slowly the procession wended its way to the solemn notes of the 'Funeral March' until it reached the steps of Frogmore. One commentator, who watched the gun carriage pass stated that it was almost impossible to believe that in that tiny coffin, which looked like that of a child, were the last remains of the world's greatest Empress. The King had ordered that the route of the procession should be via the Long Walk so that as many people as possible could pay their last respects to his mother, and there was a great, silent crowd.

Frogmore had been a special place for the Queen and during the remainder of her lifetime after she had been widowed there was rarely a day went by,

The exterior of the Frogmore Mausoleum.   *Navy & Army Illustrated*

The Albert Memorial in the Mausoleum at Frogmore.   *Navy & Army Illustrated*

when she was resident in Windsor, that she did not visit the last resting place of her husband in the Prince Consort's Mausoleum. All of the mourners who walked behind the gun carriage on this final journey would have, at one time or another, accompanied the Queen on at least one of these many visits. The procession was led by the King and the Kaiser and it was noted by some observers that Queen Alexandra was walking along holding the Duke of York's hand.

When the party reached Frogmore they were confronted with the great mausoleum, above the door of which Victoria had had the following words placed: 'His mourning widow, Victoria the Queen, directed that all that is mortal of Prince Albert be placed in the sepulchre. AD 1862. Farewell beloved! Here, at last, will I rest with thee; with thee in Christ I will rise again'.

Frogmore

Many years earlier before the death of the Duchess of Kent, the Queen's mother, Frogmore was regarded as one of the most charming of established residences and estates. However, in the later years of Queen Victoria's reign it had become a dull and desolate place. An external view of the house showed that the main centre core of the building was flanked by two low wings and along the front on the ground floor there were eight windows and a porticoed front door.

The house was approached by a broad gravel drive which was lined with evergreens and on reaching the front the eye alighted on a large oval bed of rhododendron. The whole area was surrounded by black painted railings which were 'touched by gold' as a contemporary report says. Trees and shrubs seemed to flourish here maybe because of the dampish atmosphere due to the small lake at the back of the house. Beside the front door stood a set of horse steps which betrayed an equine interest and nearby a little path led through the shrubbery to the Tea House, but more of this later.

The house was also very convenient, being situated within easy walking distance of Windsor Castle, and had become a popular retreat and pleasure ground for many monarchs and their families. It was in this house that Lord Louis Mountbatten, one of Queen Victoria's great-grandchildren. was born in the early morning of 25th June, 1900. After his birth the Queen especially asked that the name Albert be added to his four others and he was christened Louis Francis Albert Victor Nicholas, later known within the family as 'Dickie' so as not to confuse him with other royal relations who shared the same christian names.

Over the latter part of her life the Queen's mother had become more and more closely associated with Frogmore and it was decided that after her death a mausoleum should be erected to her in the beautiful grounds of this, her former home. Also it was here that her remains were to stay. The Queen and Prince Albert took a very keen interest in the siting and building of the Duchess of Kent's last resting place. Plans were drawn up and the structure built in a sympathetic style, so much so that on 20th August, 1861 the Prince Consort wrote in a letter to their eldest daughter Princess Victoria that, 'the mausoleum has become very beautiful, and just what it should be - appropriate, pleasing, solemn; not doleful or at all repellent'.

The mausoleum for the Duchess of Kent was built in the manner of an Indian temple having a cupola roof supported on 16 granite columns and surrounded by a terraced walk. A statue of the Duchess was placed in a niche and a bust of the Queen's half-sister in a glass case.

The building was constructed of Portland stone and the approach is via a little bridge which crosses part of the lake and is partly hidden by weeping willow trees. The final approach to the building is up a double flight of steps which lead up to a pair of heavy oaken doors.

Less than four months after her mother's death Victoria was to be faced with having to choose a site where the mortal remains of the Prince Consort would be laid to rest. Naturally she chose somewhere that was very close to her heart and near to her principal home. Frogmore was the obvious choice. Various designs for a mausoleum were submitted and the one that the Queen chose was described as being 'exceedingly fine and original', not, as suggested by some commentators and observers, copied from some continental model. The building is large and measures 80 feet long by 70 feet wide.

The Queen instructed that the mausoleum should be built of the finest quality materials that were available and that there should be room within it, set aside, so that she could join her husband when the time came. When she laid down this stipulation she could not have realised that this would be not be until almost 40 years later.

An enormous white marble sarcophagus was ordered, but was not ready in time for the interment of the Prince on 18th December, 1862 and on the day a temporary stone one was used. When the sarcophagus was completed a statue of the recumbent Prince Consort by Baron Marochetti was placed on the top of it and beside it was the empty space for his wife. A picture of this tomb can be seen on page 84.

The final resting place of the Prince Consort was naturally larger and more imposing and designed to be more splendid and elegant than that of the Duchess of Kent. It was built in the shape of a cross and was lighted by eight windows set into the blue and gold cupola, windows which shed their light on the white marble pillars, the golden walls, the inlaid floor, the frescos and stained glass.

There were also four bronze and gold oil lamps which were given by the Prince of Wales. In the centre of the roof was an octagonal tower with a dome sheathed in copper with a square tower on top of it surmounted by a gilt cross.

The exterior was faced with the finest Aberdeen and Guernsey granite and with various different coloured stone from around the country. The mausoleum was approached by a fine flight of stone steps guarded by two bronze figures of angels, one holding a trumpet and the other a sword.

Beneath the dome was placed the sarcophagus which was supported by four bronze angels. At the east end of the mausoleum an altar was placed with a large painting fixed above it showing Christ coming out of the tomb, the Roman soldiers falling at his feet under their shields, overcome by His triumph over death.

One of the most tender details can be found in an alcove where there was placed a touching monument of two recumbent figures, those of Princess Alice, the late Grand Duchess of Hesse, lying as though asleep, and the little child she lost her own life in trying to save nestled in the hollow of her arm. She died in 1878. Above her memorial hangs a picture of the Virgin and Child with St Joseph and the shepherds paying homage. Other statues which were placed within the burial chamber represent the biblical figures, David, Solomon, Isaiah and Daniel.

The Queen and her children often drove or walked through the grounds of Windsor Castle and often visited the mausoleum. Frequently she would go there and sit and pray. Annually, on the anniversary of the Prince Consort's death, 14th December (Princess Alice of Hesse also died on the same day 10 years later), all the members of the Royal Family who were in Great Britain at the time attended a memorial service in the mausoleum. It was on this one day a year that the general public were admitted to see the tomb, but this was strictly controlled by a ticket-only admission system.

On this day every year the whole of the Court and the Royal Household were expected to wear mourning all day, which one assumes to mean sombre clothes and black arm bands. The day was as if held in suspension, no business was conducted and no functions were held. Apart from the one short drive from the Castle to the mausoleum at Frogmore the Queen 'took no air' that day (she either drove or walked out most days for exercise) and spent the time alone in her rooms. Not even the members of the Royal Family were granted an audience that day, and the only time they saw her was at the memorial service.

There were so many happy memories for Victoria at Frogmore. Memories ranging through from her childhood with her mother, to her adolescence and then becoming a young bride with her husband Prince Albert. She loved the place greatly and it was very common practice for her, when she was in residence at Windsor, to spent her mornings in the grounds of Frogmore House. Here in the grounds was a veranda-surrounded bungalow near two large oak trees which are said to date back to the times of the Crusaders, and it was here she would spent her mornings. The bungalow soon became known as the Queen's Tea Pavilion.

The Tea House was built of wood and 'splatter work' and had a conical roof of red clay tiles. The interior was furnished in oak and the walls were covered with a flower-patterned wallpaper representing trellis work. On the ceiling was painted a billowing cloudy scene with a flying swallow painted in the centre. To one side of the bungalow was a roofed open passage which led to a smaller building which was a little preparation kitchen.

On fine days the Queen would often go to the bungalow for breakfast and it was to this little kitchen that the chefs in the main kitchen in the Castle sent down a selection of cooked breakfast dishes loaded in a horse-drawn, warmed fourgon. When eating here the Queen was always served entirely on silver. She sometimes sat within the house and sometimes under the shade of the two giant oak trees, while two pipers played merry Scots tunes.

Outside the bungalow stood a small polished grey granite fountain which assisted in supplying the water to the building. Other items such as cream, milk

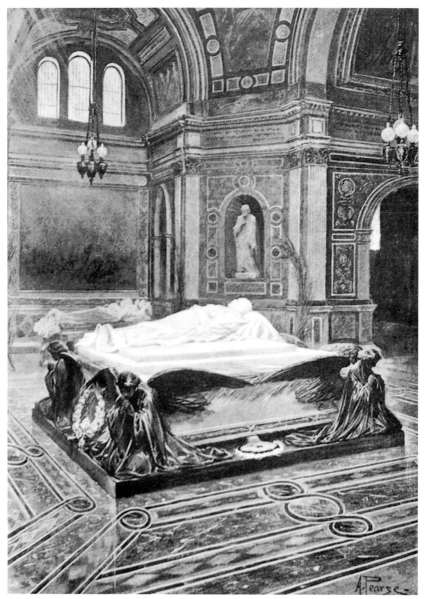

The Royal Tomb within the Mausoleum at Frogmore with the space alongside Albert for Victoria.

and butter were brought fresh from the dairy opposite which for many years was run by two very efficient Scots ladies named Stoddart.

A little way behind the Tea House and hidden behind the trees was a light iron fence which enclosed an area where the two mausoleums were constructed. The grounds of Frogmore House are beautiful and peaceful and not in the least morbid, possibly due to the fact that both of the mausoleums are surrounded by trees and so are hidden from the direct gaze of the garden visitor.

Laid to Rest

As stated earlier in this book at 3 o'clock the procession, with the Royal coffin placed on a gun carriage, left the Chapel of St George and slowly made its way through the grounds of Windsor Great Park to the Prince Consort's mausoleum at Frogmore. All had been made ready within the building to accommodate the Royal remains. The sarcophagus which was to hold the Queen's coffin lay beside that of the Prince Consort and was surrounded by a temporary platform which, for the occasion, had been covered with purple drapes over which was laid a grey cloth. The wall lamps were lit and the interior was heavily bedecked everywhere with white flowers and the atmosphere was heady with their perfume.

On reaching Frogmore the coffin was removed from the gun carriage and then slowly carried up the steps towards the mausoleum and on through the porchway into the building. While this was happening a mournful lament was being played by a group of Scots pipers. The choir from St George's Chapel then filed in and took their appointed places on the left hand side of the mausoleum. Once in place the choir chanted two opening sentences after which they sang the anthem *Yea, though I walk*, which was set to Sir Arthur Sullivan's music.

The service of interment began with the Bishop of Winchester reading the Prayer of Committal from the standard Form of Service to be found in the *Book of Common Prayer*. Then Lord Edward Pelham-Clinton, who had been the Master of the Queen's Household, was given the privilege of casting upon the Royal coffin a handful of sacred earth which had been brought from the Holy Land. The Bishop then read a prayer and the choir sang the *Kyrie Eleison* ('Lord have Mercy, Christ have Mercy, Lord have Mercy'), and then the Lord's Prayer. This was followed by intercessions which were led by the Dean of Windsor, then a hymn, the reading of the special Collect, and after that the singing of another anthem. The service concluded with a blessing which was given by the Bishop and the simple service closed with the choir singing Stainer's *Sevenfold Amen*.

At the end of the service and before leaving the Chapel the King then knelt for some time in prayer by the side of the tomb of his mother, after which those present filed past and looked one last time upon the coffin of the last great Queen Empress before they left the mausoleum.

In a break with a centuries-old tradition neither the Lord Steward nor the Lord Chamberlain of the Queen's Royal Household broke their wands of office over the coffin, and this quaint ceremony, which for centuries had always been scrupulously carried out in almost every monarchical country, had been allowed to drop in Great Britain. Queen Victoria's funeral was the first funeral of an English Sovereign at which this had been omitted. The Chamberlain of HRH The Duchess of Teck broke his wand over the coffin at her funeral. Probably the omission in the case of Queen Victoria's wanded stewards was due to the fact that for an English Sovereign the whole act would now be meaningless because, by an Act of Parliament, the offices of the Lord Chamberlain and the Lord Steward were no longer vacated upon the death of the Monarch. In the case of the Duchess of Teck's household the office came to an end.

Once the Service of Committal was finished the members of the Royal Family, and those who had been close to the Queen , mounted the platform and filed slowly past the open tomb. The ceremony having taken place the members of the Royal party passed through the mausoleum and on out into the grounds of Frogmore House. When the mourners left the building, on looking across the park they noticed that while they had been inside the whole area had been covered with a thin layer of snow. The Queen had requested a white funeral and this seemed that the whole world was making this moving final tribute to her.

The funeral party now returned to Windsor Castle and many of the distinguished official guests took their leave of the King and Queen that afternoon. That evening there were only 23 people seated in the Royal dining room. The following day the Emperor of Germany left and the King accompanied him as far as Marlborough House, then after taking luncheon the Emperor left for Germany during the afternoon. The King, the Queen and other members of the Royal Family stayed in Windsor for a further three days. On Thursday 7th February they returned to their home in Marlborough House to prepare themselves to take up the highest office in the land.

The reign of the great Queen Empress was over, the Victorian Age, the age of development, invention and innovation had come to an end and the Edwardian Era had begun. After many years in waiting King Edward had ascended to the throne and was crowned in Westminster Abbey on 26th June, 1902. By this time Edward was in his 60th year, and he was to hold the highest office in the land for less than nine years, passing away on 6th May, 1910.

Appendix

The Order of Procession

The Procession will then move in the following order :—

An Officer of the Headquarters Staff.

Bands of the Household Cavalry.

Volunteers—
    2nd South Middlesex Rifles.
    1st Middlesex Engineers.
    Tynemouth Artillery.

2

Yeomanry—

Warwickshire.

Colonial Corps—

Detachment formed under the orders of the Colonial Office and of the
Officer Commanding Provisional Battalion, Shorncliffe.

Militia—

3rd Battalion Gordon Highlanders.

3rd Battalion Royal Welsh Fusiliers.

4th Battalion Royal Irish Regiment.

4th Battalion Norfolk Regiment.

Honourable Artillery Company (Infantry Detachment).

Army Veterinary Department.

Army Pay Corps.

Army Ordnance Corps.

Army Chaplains' Department.

Royal Army Medical Corps.

Army Service Corps.

Representatives of the Indian Army, selected by the India Office.

Infantry of the Line—

4th Battalion Rifle Brigade.

Royal Irish Fusiliers.

2nd Battalion Highland Light Infantry.

4th Battalion King's Royal Rifle Corps.

Royal Fusiliers.

1st Battalion Royal Lancaster Regiment.

APPENDIX

3

Foot Guards —

    Irish Guards.

    Scots Guards.

    Coldstream Guards.

    Grenadier Guards.

Corps of Royal Engineers.

Royal Regiment of Artillery —

    Royal Garrison Artillery.

    Royal Field Artillery.

    Royal Horse Artillery.

Cavalry of the Line —

    21st Lancers.

    7th Hussars.

    2nd Dragoon Guards.

Household Cavalry —

    Royal Horse Guards.

    2nd Life Guards.

    1st Life Guards.

Royal Navy, &c. —

    Royal Marine Light Infantry.

    Royal Marine Artillery.

    Royal Navy.

The Military Attachés to the Foreign Embassies.

The Headquarters Staff of the Army and Field-Marshals —

    Field-Marshal Earl Roberts, V.C., K.G., K.P.

Band of the Royal Marine Light Infantry.

Band of the Guards.

Band of the Royal Engineers.

Band of the Royal Artillery.

4

The Earl Marshal,
The Duke of Norfolk, K.G.

Three Gold Sticks.

Lord Belper, P.C.   Duke of Buccleuch, K.G., K.T.   Earl of Waldegrave, P.C.

White Staves.

Viscount Valentia, M.P.,   Sir A. Acland Hood, Bart.,   Victor Cavendish, Esq., M.P.,
Comptroller of the Household.   Vice Chamberlain.   Treasurer of Household.

Earl of Clarendon,   Earl of Pembroke, G.C.V.O.,
Lord Chamberlain.   Lord Steward.

Aides-de-Camp.   Aides-de-Camp.

Colonel B. G. D. Cooke.   Colonel J. C. Cavendish.
Colonel Lord Blythswood.   Colonel Sir R. Ogilvy, Bart.
Colonel J. H. Rivett-Carnac, C.I.E.   Colonel The Duke of Northumberland, K.G.
Colonel J. Stevenson.   Colonel The Marquis of Londonderry, K.G.
Colonel The Earl of Harewood.   Colonel The Earl of Haddington.
Colonel The Duke of Beaufort.   Colonel The Viscount Galway.
Colonel C. B. Bashford.   Colonel C. P. Le Cornu, C.B.
Colonel The Earl of Cawdor.   Colonel Lord Suffield, K.C.B.
Colonel The Earl of March.   Colonel Wood Martin.
Colonel The Duke of Montrose, K.T.   Colonel W. Bell, C.B.
Brevet-Colonel T. F. D. Bridge.   Colonel W. Campbell.
Colonel H. H. Mathias, C.B.   Colonel H. G. Dixon, C.B.
Colonel W. Aitken, C.B.   Colonel G. L. C. Money, C.B., D.S.O.
Colonel E. T. Hutton, C.B.   Captain The Hon. Hedworth Lambton, R.N.
Captain Sir Edward Chichester, Bart.,   Captain Charles Campbell, C.B., D.S.O.
    C.B., C.M.G.
Captain Edmund S. Poë, M.V.O.   Captain Angus MacLeod.
Captain Count Frederick C. Metaxa.   Captain Alfred A. C. Parr.
Captain William H. May, M.V.O.   Captain George L. Atkinson.

Lt.-Col. A. Davidson,   Col. J. Brocklehurst,
    M.V.O.   M.V.O.

		Party of Non-Commissioned Officers	Gun Carriage	of the Guards and Household Cavalry.		

Lt.-Col. Hon. H. C. Legge,   Capt. F. Ponsonby,   Officer
2nd in   M.V.O.   M.V.O.   Command-
command   ing
of   Escort.
Escort.   Lt.-Col. Sir A. Bigge,   Lt.-Col. Hon. W. P.   Trumpeter.
    K.C.B., C.M.G.   Carington, C.B.

Maj.-Gen. Sir J. McNeill,   Lt.-Col. The Rt. Hon. Sir
    V.C., K.C.B., K.C.M.G.   F. I. Edwards, K.C.B.

Major Count Gleichen, C.M.G.   H.S.H. Prince Louis of Battenberg, G.C.B.
Vice-Admiral Sir J. Fullerton, K.C.V.O., C.B.   Admiral Sir M. Culme-Seymour, Bart., G.C.B.

5

| Royal |
| Standard |

borne by a Non-Commissioned Officer of the Household Cavalry.

King's A.D.C.,	H.R.H.	THE KING.	H.I.M.	King's Equerry,
Major-Gen.	The Duke of		The German	Capt. Holford.
Brabazon, C.B.	Connaught.		Emperor.	

Field Officer	The Master of the	General von Scholl.	Silver Stick.
in Waiting.	Horse, The Duke of		
	Portland, K.G.		

H.M. The King of the Hellenes.   H.M. The King of Portugal.

| H.R.H. Prince Henry of | H.R.H. Prince Christian of | H.R.H. The Grand Duke |
| Prussia. | Schleswig-Holstein. | of Hesse. |

| H.H. Prince Albert of | H.R.H. Prince Arthur of | H.R.H. The Duke of Saxe- |
| Schleswig-Holstein. | Connaught. | Coburg and Gotha. |

| H.R.H. The Crown Prince of | H.I. & R.H. The Crown Prince | H.R.H. The Duke of Sparta. |
| Roumania. | of Germany. | |

| H.R.H. Prince Charles of | H.R.H. The Crown Prince of | H.S.H. The Prince Hohenlohe- |
| Denmark. | Denmark. | Langenburg. |

| H.R.H. The Crown Prince of | H.I. & R.H. the Archduke | H.I.H. The Hereditary Grand |
| Norway and Sweden. | Francis Ferdinand of Austria. | Duke Michael. |

| H.R.H. The Duke of Aosta. | H.R.H. The Crown Prince of | H.R.H. The Duke of Saxony. |
| | Siam. | |

| H.R.H. The Hereditary Grand | H.R.H. Prince Arnulf of | H.R.H. The Duke Robert of |
| Duke of Baden. | Bavaria. | Wurtemberg. |

H.R.H.	H.R.H.	H.R.H.
Prince Waldeck Pyrmont.	Prince Ernest Hohenlohe.	Prince of Hohenzollern
		and Siegmazingen.

H.R.H. The Prince Philip of	H.R.H. the Duke Adolphus	H.H. The Hereditary Prince
Saxe-Coburg.	Frederick of Mecklenburg-	of Saxe-Meiningen.
	Strelitz.	

| H.S.H. The Prince Adolph of | H.H. The Duke Ernest | H.H. Prince Frederick |
| Schaumberg-Lippe. | Gunther of Schleswig-Holstein. | Charles of Hesse. |

| H.S.H. Prince Francis of Teck. | H.S.H. The Duke of Teck. | H.H. Prince Leopold of |
| | | Saxe-Coburg. |

| Mehemet Ali. | H.S.H. Prince Ernest of | H.H. Prince Henry Reuss XXX. |
| | Saxe-Altenburg. | |

| The Duke of Fife. | H.S.H. Prince Alexander of Teck. |

The Crown Equerry,
Major-General Sir H. Ewart.

Deputation of Officers of the German Army.

Officers of the Suite of The German Emperor.

G

1st Carriage.—

The Queen.
H.R.H. Princess Louise, Duchess of Fife.
H.R.H. Princess Victoria.
H.R.H. Princess Charles of Denmark.

2nd Carriage.—

H.M. The King of The Belgians.
H.R.H. Princess Christian of Schleswig-Holstein.
H.R.H. Princess Louise, Duchess of Argyll.
H.R.H. Princess Henry of Battenberg.

3rd Carriage.—

H.I.H. The Duchess of Saxe-Coburg and Gotha
H.R.H. The Duchess of Connaught.
H.R.H. The Duchess of Albany.
H.S.H. Princess Adolph of Schaumberg-Lippe.

4th Carriage.—

Field-Marshal H.R.H. The Duke of Cambridge.
Field-Marshal H.H. Prince Edward of Saxe-Weimar, K.P., G.C.B.
Field-Marshal Right Hon. Viscount Wolseley, K.P., G.C.B., Gold Stick.

5th Carriage.—

The Duchess of Buccleuch, Mistress of the Robes.
The Countess of Lytton, Lady in Waiting.
Miss Phipps, Woman of the Bedchamber.
(All to Her late Majesty.)
Lord Lawrence.

6th Carriage.—

Lady Suffield, Lady in Waiting to The Queen.
Miss Knollys, Woman of the Bedchamber to The Queen.
Lord Churchill.

Non-Commissioned Officers and Men of German Army Deputation.

Closing Escort.

On the arrival at Paddington Station the Coffin will be removed from the Gun Carriage by the Bearer Party of Non-Commissioned Officers of the Guards and Household Cavalry.

At one o'clock the train conveying the Royal Remains will leave for Windsor.

On arriving at Windsor the Coffin will be removed from the carriage by a second Bearer Party of Non-Commissioned Officers of the Guards and Household Cavalry, and placed upon a Gun Carriage, and the Crown and Cushion, the Regalia and Insignia of the Garter laid, as before, thereon.

Naval and Military Guards of Honour will be mounted at Windsor.

The procession to St. George's Chapel will move in the following order :—

Escort of the Life Guards.

Pursuivants of Arms.

General Pole-Carew and Staff.

7

Aides-de-Camp.

Colonel B. G. D. Cooke.
Colonel Lord Blythswood.
Colonel J. H. Rivett-Carnac, C.I.E.
Colonel J. Stevenson.
Colonel The Earl of Harewood.
Colonel The Duke of Beaufort.
Colonel C. B. Bashford.
Colonel The Earl of Cawdor.
Colonel The Earl of March.
Colonel The Duke of Montrose, K.T.
Brevet-Colonel T. F. D. Bridge.
Colonel H. H. Mathias, C.B.
Colonel W. Aitken, C.B.
Colonel E. T. Hutton, C.B.
Captain Sir Edward Chichester, Bart.,
  C.B., C.M.G.
Captain Edmund S. Poë, M.V.O.
Captain Count Frederick C. Metaxa.
Captain William H. May, M.V.O.

Colonel J. C. Cavendish.
Colonel Sir R. Ogilvy, Bart.
Colonel The Duke of Northumberland, K.G.
Colonel The Marquis of Londonderry, K.G.
Colonel The Earl of Haddington.
Colonel The Viscount Galway.
Colonel C. P. Le Cornu, C.B.
Colonel Lord Suffield, K.C.B.
Colonel Wood Martin.
Colonel W. Bell, C.B.
Colonel W. Campbell.
Colonel H. G. Dixon, C.B.
Colonel G. L. C. Money, C.B., D.S.O.
Captain The Hon. Hedworth Lambton, R.N.
Captain Charles Campbell, C.B., D.S.O.

Captain Angus MacLeod.
Captain Alfred A. C. Parr.
Captain George L. Atkinson.

Deputations from two German Regiments.

Adjutant General.   Quartermaster General.

Commander in Chief.

The Massed Bands.

The Heralds.

Ulster King of Arms.   Lyon King of Arms.

Norroy King of Arms.

The Earl Marshal.

The Gold Sticks.

The White Staves.

The Lord Chamberlain.   The Lord Steward.

Lt.-Col. A. Davidson,
  M.V.O.

Lt.-Col. Hon. H. C.
  Legge, M.V.O.

2nd
in command
of Escort.   Lt.-Col. Sir A. Bigge,
                  K.C.B., C.M.G.

Maj.-Gen.
Sir J. McNeill, V.C.,
  K.C.B., K.C.M.G.

Bearer Party of Non-Commissioned

Gun
Carriage

Officers of the Guards and Household Cavalry.

Col. J. Brocklehurst,
  M.V.O.

Capt. F. Ponsonby,
  M.V.O.

Lt.-Col.   Officer
Hon. W. P. Carington,   Commanding
  C.B.   Escort.
                            Trumpeter.

Lt.-Col.
The Rt. Hon.
Sir F. I. Edwards.
  K.C.B.

Major Count Gleichen, C.M.G.
Vice-Admiral Sir J. Fullerton, K.C.V.O., C.B.

H.S.H. Prince Louis of Battenberg, G.C.B.
Admiral Sir M. Culme-Seymour, Bart., G.C.B.

8

```
Royal
Standard
```

borne by a Non-Commissioned Officer of the Household Cavalry.

King's A.D.C..   H.R.H. The   THE KING.   H.I.M. The   King's Equerry,
Major-Gen.   Duke of   German   Capt. Holford.
Brabazon, C.B.   Connaught.   Emperor.

Field Officer   The Master of   General von   Silver Stick,
in Waiting.   the Horse, The   Scholl.
    Duke of
    Portland, K.G.

H.M. The King of the Hellenes.   H.M. The King of Portugal.

H.R.H. Prince Henry of   H.R.H. Prince Christian of   H.R.H. The Grand Duke
Prussia.   Schleswig-Holstein.   of Hesse.

H.H. Prince Albert of   H.R.H. Prince Arthur of   H.R.H. The Duke of
Schleswig-Holstein.   Connaught.   Saxe-Coburg and Gotha.

H.R.H. The Crown Prince of   H.I. & R.H. The Crown Prince   H.R.H. The Duke of
Roumania.   of Germany.   Sparta.

H.R.H. Prince Charles of   H.R.H. The Crown Prince of   H.S.H. The Prince Hohenlohe-
Denmark.   Denmark.   Langenburg.

H.R.H. The Crown Prince of   H.I. & R.H. The Archduke   H.I.H. The Hereditary Grand
Norway and Sweden.   Francis Ferdinand of Austria.   Duke Michael.

H.R.H. The Duke of Aosta.   H.R.H. The Crown Prince of   H.R.H. The Duke of Saxony.
    Siam.

H.R.H. The Hereditary Grand   H.R.H. Prince Arnulf of   H.R.H. The Duke Robert of
Duke of Baden.   Bavaria.   Wurtemberg.

H.R.H. Prince Waldeck   H.R.H. Prince Ernest   H.R.H. Prince of
Pyrmont.   Hohenlohe.   Hohenzollern.

H.R.H. The Prince Philip   H.R.H. The Duke Adolphus   H.H. The Hereditary Prince
of Saxe-Coburg.   Frederick of Mecklenburg-   of Saxe-Meiningen.
    Strelitz.

H.S.H. The Prince Adolph of   H.H. The Duke Ernest   H.H. Prince Frederick Charles
Schaumberg-Lippe.   Gunther of Schleswig-   of Hesse.
    Holstein.

Mehemet Ali.   H.S.H. The Duke of Teck.   H.H. Prince Henry
    Reuss XXX.

H.S.H. Prince Francis of Teck.   H.H. Prince Leopold of Saxe-Coburg

The Duke of Fife.   H.S.H. Prince Ernest of   H.S.H. Prince Alexander
    Saxe-Altenburg.   Teck.

9

Representatives of Foreign States—

AMBASSADORS.

Turkey .. .. { Turkhan Pasha.
                                    { Alexander Caratheodori Pasha.
France .. .. Vice-Admiral Bienaimé.
United States .. .. The Honourable Joseph H. Choate.
Spain .. .. The Duke of Mandas and Villanueva.
Japan .. .. Baron Hayashi.

ENVOYS EXTRAORDINARY AND MINISTERS PLENIPONTENTIARY.

Persia .. .. General Mirza Mahommed Ali Khan,
                                    Ala-es-Saltaneh.
Guatemala .. .. Señor Don Fernando Cruz.
Nicaragua .. .. Señor Don Cristano Medina.
Paraguay .. .. Señor Don Eusebio Machain.
Chile .. .. Señor Don Domingo Gana.
Argentine Republic .. .. Señor Don Florencio L. Dominguez.
Switzerland .. .. Mons. Charles D. Bourcart.
Netherlands .. .. Baron de Hardenbrock de Bergambacht.
Mexico .. .. Señor Don Sebastian Mier.
Servia .. .. M. Mijatovitch.
Brazil.. .. .. Señor Don J. A. Nabuco.
Uruguay .. .. Señor Don Alfonso de Zumaran.
Bulgaria .. .. Count de Bourboulon.
Corea .. .. Tchin Pomm Ye.
Ecuador .. .. M. Homère Morla.
Hanover .. .. Colonel Baron von Klenck.
Luxemburg .. .. Count d'Assembourg.
Mecklenburg-Schwerin .. .. .. Count von Hardenburg.
Monaco .. .. The Count Balny d'Avricourt.
Oldenburg .. .. Count von Wedel.

Suites of the Royal Representatives.

Suites of Representatives of Foreign States.

Non-Commissioned Officers and Men of the German Deputation.

Gentlemen at Arms with their Axes reversed.

Yeomen of the Guard with their Partizans reversed.

Bibliography and Acknowledgements

The Illustrated London News
The Army and Navy Gazette
The Navy & Army Illustrated
The Strand Magazine
The Times
The Shy Princess by David Duff.
'The Private Life of Queen Victoria', by one of Her Majesty's Servants
The Archives of the Chapel of St George Windsor
The Archives of the Chapel Royal
The Admiralty Library, Portsmouth
The Royal Archives, Windsor Castle
The staff of the Chapel Royal, Hampton Court
The Portsmouth News
The Hampshire Telegraph
Gosport's Railway Era, by G.A. Alcock
Branch Lines Around Gosport, by Vic Mitchell and Keith Smith (Middleton Press)
Rails to the Yards, published by the Gosport Railway Society
Windsor to Slough: A Royal Branch Line by C.R. Potts (Oakwood Press)
The Archives of the Gosport Railway Society
J. Horne
Doug Scorey for his advice and encouragement.

The railway viaduct on the GWR Windsor branch line.
From a drawing by Daphne Fido